The Importance of Being Earnest

OSCAR WILDE

The Importance of Being Earnest

EDITED BY

VINCENT F. HOPPER and
GERALD B. LAHEY

New York University

WITH A NOTE ON THE STAGING

GEORGE L. HERSEY

Bucknell University

ILLUSTRATIONS BY

FRITZ KREDEL

BARRON'S EDUCATIONAL SERIES

Great Neck, New York

The Importance of Being Earnest

THEATRE CLASSICS FOR THE MODERN READER

To reproduce the values and effects of the theatre on the printed page is the ambitious aim of this series of the classics of the stage. Although good plays have always been read as well as acted, few playwrights before the era of Ibsen and Shaw have ever written with any public other than the theatre audience sharply in their minds. In consequence, the reader of older plays is usually required to supply his own visualizing of the staging and his own interpretation of stage action and even the manner of the delivery of the lines themselves. Frequently he is also required to put up with abbreviations and other space-saving printing devices.

This modern reader's edition of theatre classics vitalizes the outstanding plays of the past with the kind of eye-pleasing text and the kinds of reading and acting guides to which today's reader is accustomed in good published editions of twentieth century dramas. The text itself has not been altered except for occasional modernizations of spelling and punctuation (common to all modern editions of earlier works) and the rare use of italics for emphasis when the reading of a line is not immediately clear. Essentially, that is, the author's text is as he wrote it. Added to it are descriptions of scenes and costumes, indications of expression and action, and explanation of words and references not readily comprehensible.

The illustrations should aid immeasurably in visualizing the play. A description of the original staging, stage conditions, and stage techniques is provided partly as still another aid to visualization but principally to show how the playwright adapted his materials to suit the particular stage conventions of his time. Companioning each play are also a sketch of the author's life, an analysis of the play, and a selective bibliography to make this as much an all-in-one edition as possible.

THE PLAYWRIGHT

The nineteenth century opened and closed on the notes of dandyism and scandal. Byron, friend of the fashion-arbiter Beau Brummel, was the type of the athletic, satanic dandy touched with melancholy; Wilde that of the aesthetic, sybaritic dandy, graced with supercilious cynicism. At opposite ends of the century, their colorful personalities were the scandalous spectres that haunted their respective generations. Wilde had said that history is mere gossip, and scandal is gossip made tedious by moralizing. In *The Importance of Being Earnest* one of the characters intimates that gossip is the spice that makes much history readable. Both Byron and Wilde were brilliant literary satirists, whose provocative wit and insolent, invincible gaiety punctured the moral pretensions and distressed the domestic sanctities of their day. Both were figures with a strong theatrical bent which disposed them to translate into action portions of their artistic imaginations.

Needless to say, others furnished scandals in the course of the century; but the chief scandals were ecclesiastical and theological; England in the forties was shocked at clergymen who, becoming too religious, threatened her with superstition; and in the sixties with clergymen who, becoming too reflective, threatened her with skepticism. But these were scandals of the mind. Byron and Wilde were looked upon as monstrous fleshly transgressors of the moral law; the former for having iniquitous relations with his married half-sister, the latter prosecuted and imprisoned for homosexual offenses in distant days before an Archbishop of Canterbury had made comforting distinctions between sin and crime.

Wilde, like Byron, was the child of eccentric and turbulent parents. If Byron was the Romantic movement of the early century vanishing like a bursting rocket, Wilde was the Aesthetic movement of the *fin de siècle* expiring

9

amidst flashes of wit and cries of shame. But between Byron, author of the satiric and scandalous *Don Juan,* and Wilde, creator of the "decadent" and shocking *Picture of Dorian Gray,* stands the sturdy figure of Queen Victoria, emblematic of the nineteenth-century middle-class ascendency, together with its code of prudish propriety, of righteous respectability. Macaulay, friend of Sir William Wilde, Oscar's father, had commented in the 1840's in a review of Byron's life on the periodic fits of indignation to which John Bull was subject. Macaulay, himself something of a moralist, had spoken of the public disposition to be shocked at exceptional personalities as the means whereby the "savage envy of aspiring dunces is gratified by the agonies of such a spirit . . ." But whereas Byron had quarrelled with a remarkably tolerant Regency society, presumably dominated by an aristocratic sense of moral laissez-faire and had gone into voluntary exile, Wilde shocked and outraged the age of Victoria, not that of Florizel. The wages of that sin were two years at hard labor.

The wealthy, sub-aristocratic society which was riding the tides of the new industrial wealth had in a manner made respectability its watchword and talisman. Aware of its inferiority to the aristocracy in point of pedigree, taste, and manners, it sought to show its superiority to a "corrupt" aristocracy, not only in wealth but in morals; it comforted its uneasy relation to aristocracy (and its own aristocratic indifference to poverty) by asserting its semi-divine calling to respectability, thus justifying the ways of Mammon to man. Its moral code insisted on the purity and innocence of domestic life and private conduct, together with a utilitarian and pragmatic standard for political and economic behavior. Wilde had the happy insolence to affront all of the values and sensibilities of this society. He made the term "middle-class" a satiric epithet for the dull, unimaginative, hypocritical, stale, mid-century Philistine, a term of disparagement for a class supremely deficient in appreciation of the art of living and the living arts.

Wilde's preparation for his double role of apostle to

and scandal of the Philistines began, like all really good preparations, with his parents. They in their way provided a sort of ironic foreshadowing of the sensational events of his own life. His mother was a woman with remarkable pretensions both social and political. The poet Aubrey de Vere noted that "she liked to make a sensation." Others noted in her an amusing mixture of "nonsense and some genius." Whether presiding over her salon at No. 1 Merrion Square in Dublin or later at her London residence, she was in appearance like a slightly over-dressed tragedy-queen in a provincial theatre. She was formidable in bulk (a trait inherited by her son, Oscar) and according to Shaw a victim of acromegaly, with enormous splayed extremities of the limbs, the huge hands fumbling uncertainly towards objects they could not quite grasp. At times her appearance oscillated between that of the tragedy queen and a gypsy tea-room reader who was heavily be-brooched, be-spangled, over-ornamented with huge bracelets and pins, over-dressed in tiers of differing textures, including red shawls; she appeared to be "operating" a parlor for occult practices, rather than entertaining her menage. Her son was later to speak of a woman who aimed at holding a salon but who only succeeded in opening a restaurant. Having in mind her late suppers and plentiful supply of spirits, a menage described by Lord Alfred Douglas as "boozy and boisterous," Wilde was very probably thinking of his mother's Dublin and London conversational carnivals. Shaw has described them as impossibly dreary; not even Wilde's presence in lilac shirts and heliotrope flowing ties quite redeemed them. Yet in a way the mother was not without definite ideas of salon conversation, laying much stress upon the wit of the epigram and the paradox. Considering her extravagant eccentricity in clothes and manner, Wilde's emergence as the "Professor" of Aesthetics during and after his Oxford sojourn is possibly an extension and a refinement of the maternal manner.

In her journalistic and public career, Wilde's mother was something between a literary priestess and a political prophetess; she was one of the most ardent poetic voices of the Young Ireland movement for political independence; one of her prose writings which suggested the propriety of muskets and street barricades brought her editor Gavan Duffy and his *Nation* newspaper into conflict with the law, charged with sedition. Her equally flamboyant son was to lead a Young England movement of sorts, an aesthetic movement against the harsh utilitarian ethos of Victorian commercialism, against the narrow, high-and-dry type of Victorian character. Of this movement, known as the Aesthetic movement or the Art for Art's sake movement, Walter Pater was the philosopher; Ruskin, the evangelist; and Wilde, the popular propagandist and publicity agent.

If the mother, a social celebrity and literary agitator, prefigured the aesthetic missionary, the conduct of the father foreshadowed the scandalous tendencies of the son—as in the parallel case of Byron's father. Sir William Wilde, besides being a scholar and antiquarian, was also a brilliant surgeon and physician, treating diseases of the eye and ear: to this extent unlike the son, a maker of dramatic delights for the eye and ear. The father anticipated the moral waywardness of the son. The notorious irregularity of Sir William's sexual conduct and the resultant regularity of illegitimate issue were the origin of much unsavory Dublin humor. Like his son he was the center of a court action lurid with sexual implications which turned upon the issue of libel; like his son, his loss of the case (in the instance of the father, a technical loss involving "costs") marked the beginning of his fall from the height of his achievement. The son's sexual offenses looked in another direction. Sir William had operated on Bernard Shaw's father for a squint so successfully that, as Shaw tells us, his father "squinted the other way all the rest of his life." Nature, mindful of Sir William's satyr-like pursuit and capture of ladies, intervened in a compensating mood at the birth of his son, whose disposition in sexual matters squinted the other way. The errors of the father were avenged in his son. One wonders also about the moral as well as biological heredity; young Oscar was a boy of about ten years at the Portora Royal School—the "Eton of Ireland"—at the time of his father's notorious trial and must have been subject to considerable psychic harassment at the torrid disclosures concerning his father. Did this fact, added to his inheritance from the mother of a curiously ponderous, epicene body, contribute to his sexual aberrations?

Any sketch of Wilde falls naturally into three sections: a period of preparation, a period of notoriety, and finally a period of brilliant dramatic achievement followed sharply by personal decline. Born in October of 1854, preceding his great fellow Dubliner Shaw by two years, Wilde in 1864 entered the Portora Royal School at Enniskillen. Somewhat loutish and overgrown for his age, he was noted for a complete indifference to sports and games. A precocious reader, interested in flowers and solitude, he behaved as a schoolboy much like an adult; later, as an adult, his mood and outlook were those of the invincibly gay, perennial undergraduate. Wilde always maintained that the only proper form of exercise was to talk, not walk. Apart from riding, he later admitted that his only sport was dominoes at sidewalk cafés in Paris; football he declared to be a fine game for rough girls. It was an unusual attitude for one who was early distinguished for his proficiency in the language and culture of the Greeks who worshipped the comely athlete. Indeed Wilde's profession of indolence was something of an affectation; his pose of excessive lassitude and languor a form of rebellion against the furiously bustling and hustling Victorian Babbitt. Actually Wilde must have done a good deal of reading and done it with more than ordinary care. As a writer he liked to describe himself as studying one of his own poems all morning, removing a comma at noon, and then putting it back late in the afternoon. Or profess to fatigue from having sat up all night with an ailing primrose. In actual fact his application must have been considerable.

From Portora Royal, Wilde went to Trinity College, Dublin, the Alma Mater of Congreve and Goldsmith. Besides holding a scholarship at Trinity, Wilde won the Berkeley Gold Medal for Greek, his special interest being the Greek comic poets. Besides the Greeks, Wilde at Trinity came under the influence of a man who studied the past in the spirit of a scientist and the present as an artist—the Reverend John Portland Mahaffy, professor of ancient history. Absorbed in methods of social advancement, Mahaffy studied the art of polite conversation as an actor cons his script. He impressed upon Wilde the art of snobbery and the art of social maneuver, especially emphasizing superciliousness of manner and conversation as a gentlemanly accomplishment. When Gerald Arbuthnot says to Lord Illingworth in *A Woman of No Importance,* ". . . but I should never be able to talk as you do. I don't know how to talk," the latter, perhaps echoing Professor Mahaffy, says, "Oh! talk to every woman as if you loved her, and to every man as if he bored you, and at the end of your first season you will have the reputation of possessing the most perfect social tact." Also at Trinity during Wilde's time was a man named Carson, who was notable for trailing Wilde in the honors ratings, trailing but never overtaking him. Carson was later the prosecuting attorney who was to win a conviction against Wilde.

Wilde's prodigious memory and his natural joy in books helped him to win a scholarship for four years at Magdalen College, Oxford, where he went in 1874 at the age of 20 years. Wilde's academic success was in a way a dim foreshadowing of his literary success. He won scholarship prizes, honors at every school he attended. At Oxford, he won the coveted Newdigate prize for poetry in 1878; he likewise took First-class Honors in Classics. Despite his rare academic attainment, he always spoke slightingly of schoolmasters and formal education. Of the former he observed that those who can't learn, teach—a statement slightly revised by Shaw before issuing it as his own. Wilde complained that formal education simply taught people to remember, that nothing worth knowing could be taught at a university, where as a consequence lectures were little more than vicious, slowly eddying circles of conceited opinion. Considering that much of Wilde's poetry was a rephrasing of much nineteenth-century verse written before him, that his aesthetic theory and much of his criticism was a successful re-wording of such Oxford dons as Pater and Ruskin, and that he was to achieve his early notoriety in America and England as a lecturer, Wilde made the most of what he deplored. In fact his readiness to appropriate expressed ideas elicited special comment from the painter Whistler who congratulated him for always having the courage of other people's opinions. Wilde paid a compliment to one of Whistler's witticisms, saying, "I wish I had said that." "You will, Oscar, you will," was the tart rejoinder. Notwithstanding, Wilde's mind possessed considerable spontaneity and originality, a fact which is so evident in *The Importance of Being Earnest*.

Wilde's period of preparation ended at Oxford, where besides being cited for highest academic honors, he recited his Newdigate poem *Ravenna* in the Theatre in June of 1878. It was his maiden appearance as a creative literary figure. A disapproving critic was to say of this event that, after all, every year someone at Oxford got a Newdigate; to which Wilde replied that it was only once that the Newdigate got an Oscar. Ostensibly it is another of those poems of nineteenth-century Englishmen about the past glories of Italian cities, a nostalgic memory sharpened by their own sense of unprecedented prosperity and power. But the most vivid and lively part of the poem is a tribute to Lord Byron, thus establishing a line between their names, personal as well as historical. Besides Byron the poet, Wilde speaks even more emphatically of Byron the friend of freedom and hater of oppression:

> And Greece stood up to fight for Liberty,
> And called him from Ravenna: never knight
> Rode forth more nobly to wild scenes of fight!

· · ·

And England, too, shall glory in her son
Her warrior-poet, first in song and fight,
No longer now shall Slander's venomed spite
Crawl like a snake across his perfect name,
Or mar the lordly scutcheon of his fame . . .

It is curious that the youthful author of this animated eulogy of the name of Byron should himself have died, also an exile, with his name in still darker disrepute. As yet no English poet has placed such a chivalrous wreath upon the grave of Wilde. However, a recent biographer, Mr. Hesketh Pearson, with touches of the writer of juvenile fiction, has presented Wilde, not as the penitent pederast but as the thoroughly muscular aesthete—out-drinking, out-wrestling, out-eating, outwitting his most virile and clever adversaries of both the New and the Old Worlds—indeed almost out-acting historical probability.

Wilde's first publication, the *Poems* of 1881 (including the prize poem *Ravenna*) invites notice for its biographical as well as its literary value. In diction and themes the *Poems* are slightly tarnished now, considerably less original than the plays. However, one cannot complain of their lack of variety, especially the poems with political themes. Wilde's political moods varied somewhat capriciously. They are, however, a useful counterpoise to what is now a stereotyped view of him at this period: "the ultra-poetical, super-aesthetical, out-of-the-way young man." In this version, Wilde is the precious aesthete wearing pale lavendar gloves and hair a little too long and a trifle too decorative, with cigarette held in upturned hand a little too exquisitely; dressed in jewels and velvets he gazes through a stained-glass monocle at gatherings of sunflowers, lilies, and blue china. Notwithstanding this kind of reputation which Wilde the showman encouraged, the poems reveal in phrase and image a mind virile and vivid, quite in the style of those primary colors used for commercial advertising which Wilde was later to deplore as being startling even to deaf people.

His responses to the great movements for freedom and liberty which stirred Europe and England during the nineteenth century are seen in the poem *Ravenna,* already referred to. Here his exaltation of Byron, the liberator of the oppressed, shows at least a sentimental attachment to the old-fashioned school of the aristocratic radical, the English poet Swinburne being perhaps the nearest successor to it among Wilde's contemporaries. It was an attitude toward liberty and freedom in which enthusiasm rose in vigor as its object receded from the shores of England to the south of Europe, Greece and Italy being its favorite staging ground.

Another poem shows Wilde in the unusual role of the idealistic moralist of Empire: a few vivid lines etch the "yellow leopards" of war leaping "through the hail of screaming shell," as the highways of Empire "Shake to the tread of armed men."

> For southern wind and east wind meet
> Where, girt and crowned by sword and fire,
> England with bare and bloody feet
> Climbs the steep road of wide empire.

After meditating on the cost in terms of pain, care, and death, he asks

> What profit now that we have bound
> The whole world round with nets of gold,
> If hidden in our heart is found
> The care that groweth never old?

Then desperately hoping that the cost in human suffering and wealth is not without meaning, he concludes:

> Up the steep road must England go,
> Yet when this fiery web is spun,
> Her watchmen shall descry from far
> The young Republic like a sun
> Rise from these crimson seas of war.

The hypothetical link of causality between the last two lines is arbitrary, even for Wilde; yet they show something like Republican sentiment.

Faced directly by the issue of democracy at home, Wilde is mistrustful of its leaders:

> This England, this sea-lion of the sea,
> By ignorant demagogues is held in fee,
> Who love her not:

At another point, troubled by the thought that England was once "guardian of freedom," Wilde sees her now as the townhouse of Mammon:

> . . . . Luxury
> With barren merchandise piles up the gate
> Where noble thoughts and deeds should enter by:

This thought by the future creator of a line of magnificently supercilious and insolently luxuriant dandies is one of the ironic overtones of the little volume of 1881.

Perhaps his most decisively ambivalent poem is his *Sonnet to Liberty* whose opening lines reveal humanitarianism at the freezing point:

> Not that I love thy children, whose dull eyes
> See nothing save their own unlovely woe,
> Whose minds know nothing, nothing care to know,—

The poem goes on to affirm, Byron-like, that the reigns of terror and the anarchies of the democratic movement have but one appeal, in that they

> Mirror my wildest passion like the sea
> And give my rage a brother—!

Adding that he is supremely indifferent to despotic and kingly oppression of the people, Wilde declares of his attitude towards the street slaughter of aspiring multitudes:

> . . . I remain unmoved . . .

Then suddenly and quite ambiguously—as a possible memory of his mother's crusading fervor for freedom crosses his mind—the poem shifts its course:

> . . .   and yet, and yet,
> These Christs that die upon the barricades
> God know it, I am with them in some things.

Alongside of this disdainful condescension to the popular aspiration of his century is his sonnet *Libertatis Sacra*

Famis; after an admission that ideally he prefers equality among men, he says,

> Better the rule of One, whom all obey
> Then to let clamorous demogogues betray
> Our freedom with the kiss of anarchy.
> Wherefore, I love them not whose hands profane
> Plant the red flag upon the piled-up street
> For no right cause, beneath whose ignorant reign,
> Arts, Culture, Reverence, Honour, all things fade,
> Save Treason and the dagger of her trade,
> Or Murder with his silent bloody feet.

Despite his many vacillations, perhaps the poem that represents his feelings most truly, if most ungenerously, is his poem *Theoretikos;* conceiving of England as a "vile traffic-house," which has deserted the political ideal of freedom for commercialism, he writes that

> . . . the rude people rage with ignorant cries
> Against an heritage of centuries.
> It mars my calm: wherefore in dreams of Art
> And loftiest culture I would stand apart,
> Neither for God, nor for his enemies.

His decision is the opposite to that of Tennyson in his *Palace of Art.* Wilde turns in his ticket and stands aside from the course of history and the struggles of mankind. To refuse to join on the right or the left of the house, to aspire instead to a throne on Mt. Olympus is to recall (or anticipate) the resolutions of Stephen Dedalus in Joyce's *Portrait of the Artist as a Young Man*—the determination to ignore all mundane issues in favor of beauty. One runs the risk in thus divorcing oneself from mankind of sterilizing one's imagination; and in *The Picture of Dorian Gray* and *The Sphinx,* we have glimpses of the effect of his decision on Wilde's taste and temper.

The phrases conveying his aspiration to "stand apart" and indulge "in dreams of Art and loftiest culture are a connecting link to Wilde's rooms at Magdalen, the college whose walks and parks, courts and cloister, whose graceful Gothic tower are considered by so many as the show-window of Oxford. His panelled, ornate chambers were to become a sort of Home Office from which the young Wilde was to emerge as the front-page emissary of an Aesthetic movement, especially dedicated to the pursuit of beauty in all of its manifestations. To understand the factors generating the climate of feeling and aspiration that culminated in this movement, one must take a brief backward glance.

The Church of England, the main representative of Christianity in the England of Wilde's day, had lost its appeal to many young Englishmen. In rebellion against it in mid-century, many under the leadership of Newman had become Roman Catholics; many took the other fork in the road, the one leading to disbelief and irreligion. Indeed Wilde himself coming in the generation following this rebellion was the heir to their disenchantment; he summed up the attitude of his time: "It is enough that our fathers have believed"; then, having declared that they had "exhausted the faith-faculty of the species," Wilde asserted that "their legacy to us is the scepticism of which they were afraid."

From the beginning of the nineteenth century, two factors were operating strongly to undermine traditional belief, especially that which was rooted in Biblical Christianity. One was the great development of geology with its special implications for the story of creation in Genesis; equally strong but of wider application was the growth of the German Higher Criticism, the minute, microscopic study of the various books of the Bible, with a tendency to cast doubt on their authenticity and credibility. By 1859 these two forces had seriously undermined Victorian religious belief. In that year, when Wilde was a five-year-old Dubliner, two quite disparate publications appeared: the lesser—the FitzGerald translation of the *Rubáiyát* of Omar Khayyám, the greater—Darwin's *On the Origin of Species by Natural Selection*. The former merely gave expression to already existent disbelief, perhaps crystallizing it and sharpening it; the second gave a tremendous impulsion to disbelief, sending over the line many who were hesitating. The *Rubáiyát* recording in soothing rhythms and remote oriental imagery the disillusionments of an ancient doubter, really voiced that of the generation of its publication. During the two decades following, it went through a number of editions, becoming almost the breviary of agnosticism for the rising generation. In mild Horatian accents it suggested art, love, and good living, a quiet, refined epicurianism as the only solace of life. At its side appeared the cosmic and epic vision of Darwin, who tore up the pedigree of mankind and quietly dropped the agitated pieces into the dark backwash and abysm of time. In tones of quiet authority, Darwin informed his fellow Victorians that the many mansions of their Father's draughty house were filled with curiously pithecoid ancestors. He left it to Huxley and Bishop Wilberforce to wrangle about the validity of the new vision.

As the century wore on, it eroded the containing walls of Victorian mentality. Into the empty spiritual corridors which echoed to the retreated footsteps of the gods, new faiths and intellectual and artistic fashions crowded, seeking the allegiance of the young. Intellectually, the age splintered into a variety of movements and isms. There was the cult of the "foreigner" so alien to smug, complacent Victorianism, the victor of Waterloo. The cult included Ibsen, Baudelaire, Flaubert, the French symbolists and decadents. The French especially were to impinge sharply on Wilde's consciousness during the '80's. There was the pre-Raphaelite movement in poetry and painting, aiming at a new imaginative individualism. There was the Fabian socialism of the Wells-Shaw variety, so alien to sturdy Victorian individualism; the ardors of imperialism so distant from the insular John Bull of the earlier century; the pagan naturalism of Swinburne; the gospel of work according to Carlyle and of noble endeavor according to Ruskin were replaced by the gospel of beauty according to Pater, the gospel of pleasure and dandyism according to Wilde.

In 1773, Walter Pater published his Renaissance studies with its famous "Conclusion." He stated, in words that were a work of art in themselves, the function of art in life, of its place in satisfying the aspirations of men of imaginative gifts. His writings assumed that the old gods had departed and that the arts which had been their cup-bearers were to be elevated to the vacant thrones. Since all systems of thought and worship appeared to Pater to be but modes and fashions, he advocated the avoidance of all final formalized philosophies of existence and glorified the specific response to particular moments of beauty, to a mental life in which one was to be "forever curiously testing new opinions and courting new impressions." In this phantom existence "while all melts under our feet, we may well catch at any exquisite passion, or any contribution to knowledge that seems, by a lifted horizon, to set the spirit free for a moment, or any stirring of the senses, strange dyes, strange flowers, and curious odours. . . . Only be sure it is passion" and that it does yield "this fruit of a quickened and multiplied consciousness . . ."

Pater, aesthete and recluse, saw reality as if on a still, late autumn afternoon from the observation car at the end of a train, the shining steel threads of experience ever flowing together and vanishing, the world of experience silently slipping past, mysteriously into nothing. In dulcet, whispering tones, echoing the mood of Omar's *Rubáiyát,* he dwelt upon the ephemeral and transitory character of all creeds, of the physical world itself, which he dissolved into a temporal flux of swirling stimuli and fleeting impressions; in the middle of this foaming, bubbling current of cosmic energies, the individual stood alone, each solitary mind with nothing but "its own dream of a world." Turning from the numbing influence of habit and convention, Pater counselled the development of a sensitive, discriminating susceptibility to impressions of beauty in nature and in art; one was to use these selected moments of heightened awareness to "burn with a hard, gem-like flame" and thus to gather (as a magnifying lens the rays of the sun) rays of beauty into a burning focus of aesthetic "ecstasy," to enter into silent communion with beauty as a mystical St. Theresa might with God. The

religious revival of the '30's and '40's of the century with
its asceticism and self-mortification had offered the beauty
of holiness as the goal of moral striving; the art for art's
sake movement quite consciously transformed the asceticism into aestheticism and offered the holiness of beauty
as an alternative gospel. "Art," Wilde the disciple was to
say on his American lecture tour, "makes a sacrament of
life." In his poetry Newman had spoken of the "kindly
light" that comforted men in the "encircling gloom." For
those whose candle of faith had been extinguished by the
sharp winds of skeptical doctrine, Pater offered the "hard,
gem-like flame" that was to draw its nourishment from
perceptions of the beautiful.

Pater, the library recluse, had never dreamed of his
sacred flame burning outside the ivory tower; he sipped
life exquisitely through the colored straws of art and
books, and savored only filtered portions of reality. He
had never dreamed that his gem-like fire would be used
to ignite "flaming youth." Or that men would as a result
of his teaching pass from the lilies and languors of a
virtuous aestheticism to the roses and raptures of perverse
passion and pleasure. Or that his message concerning the
intense search for significant sensation would, in the first
instance of its development, be transformed into the intense cultivation of sensationalism in clothes and conduct. Or that his habit of quasi-monastic contemplation
would become a crusading aestheticism soliciting converts in the uniform of the dandy. Pater would have been
shocked beyond consolation could he have seen the rising
of an aesthetic school for whom

> . . . all the things of beauty burn
> With flames of evil ecstasy.

The gradual turning of the gem-like flame into one of evil
ecstasy constitutes the movement of Wilde's life. The
Aesthetic movement as it passed from the formulation of
Pater to the leadership of Wilde is symbolized in the
character of Gustave von Aschenbach of Thomas Mann's
Death in Venice, in von Aschenbach's change from the

creator and contemplator of beauty to the slave of pleasure.

As an exponent of the Aesthetic Movement, Wilde changed from an honors student in classics to a being precious in taste, paradoxical in assertion, flamboyant and flashy in clothes and conduct. By the time he had completed his studies at Oxford in 1878, Wilde had decided that though to be in society was a bore, not to be in was a tragedy. Whereas Byron had awakened to find himself famous as a poet and thereafter contrived to make himself infamous, Wilde studied the strategy of publicity into the late hours and awoke finally to find himself infamous. The second period, that of notoriety, the period of the "great splendid big boy" as Walt Whitman called him after an American interview, took shape soon after his graduation from Oxford. The splendid big boy early managed to make his way into what his plays call "the best society"; through an Oxford friend, Wilde sufficiently ingratiated himself with the Duchess of Westminster and others to make himself socially known. He immediately aimed at front-page notices and got them. As the self-possessed poseur, the flashy flaneur, the fascinating parvenu, he wandered among the titled and the talented forever admiring pedigrees, title, great houses, manner, and luxury. It was this aspect of Wilde that led his fellow-Dubliner to fight shy of him, Shaw muttering of him that there "was no snob like a Dublin snob." Wilde also made conquests of such stage celebrities as Ellen Terry and the toast of the dandies, Lily Langtry; eventually of Sarah Bernhardt. Perhaps a part of their fondness for him was their professional respect for good acting ability. Ellen Terry, whose acquaintance was wide, found him captivating; she called him the "most remarkable of men," adding that he was "more instantaneously individual and audacious than it is possible to describe." Lily Langtry sighed, "one of the most alluring voices that I have ever listened to." In reciprocal compliment Oscar announced that so infatuated was he with her perfect Hellenic profile that he intended sleeping nightly on her doorstep. Wilde's attitude towards male actors was often touched with flippant sarcasm; he noted of Henry Irving that his legs were "delicately intellectual, his left leg—a poem." Of his Hamlet, that it was magnificently funny without being vulgar. Thus Wilde made his way, both charming and infuriating; when a poet of the '90's opened a poem with the line

> I hate you with a necessary hate

he voiced not only his own probable sentiment towards Wilde but that of many others. Hated or admired, Wilde proceeded to his first achievement to get himself talked about. He became the embodiment of the art for art's sake school: his hair coiffured after the manner of the emperor Nero, his orange-colored, silk pocket-handkerchiefs, his ivory headed cane, his befrogged and befurred top-coats, his green carnation—almost his signature "buttonhole"—knee-breeches and silk stocking; *Punch* sang mockingly:

> Legs Apollo might have sighed for,
> Or great Hercules have died for,
> His knee-breeches now display.

Even at those melodramatic moments of his novels when he tells us that "Lying on the floor was a dead man . . . with a knife in his heart"—the crucial detail of the knife is delayed until we learn that the dead man lies "in evening dress." Even death was something of a dandy.

Wilde's show caught on. Years later, in 1895, in order to avoid the results of a court action against him, Wilde was urged by friends to follow the ghost of Byron into exile on the continent. Wilde rejected the suggestion, saying that only commercial travellers and missionaries went abroad. It was in something of this double capacity that Wilde in December of 1881 sailed on the Arizona for New York. He went as propagandist for the English Renaissance, his lecture-tour name for the Aesthetic Revival, and to cash in on the market the curiosity which his personal eccentricities had given rise to. Quite without critical or creative reputation other than that gained

by the publication of the *Poems* of 1881, Wilde had become the headline figure of a movement which embraced
the names of eminent critics and poets and painters:
Pater, Ruskin, Rossetti, Hunt, Millais, Whistler, etc. As
publicity, Wilde now had three international displays: his
mannerisms, dress, phrases and interests were being ridiculed in somewhat heavy Chamber-of-Commerce style in
comic opera, Gilbert's *Patience;* in a comedy, *The
Colonel;* and in the widely read, no-nonsense-about-us
magazine *Punch.* Such extravagant caricatures as Postle-
thwaite, Reginald Bunthorne, Archibald Grosvenor, Sir
Basil Giorgione, Knight of the Lily, ridiculed the supposed or real preciosities and affectations of the movement. Wilde was being laughed at by writers of considerably less wit and art than he himself possessed. In his
reference to these "advertisements" in the opening lecture
in America (*Patience* was already a flourishing "Broad-
way hit") he observed coolly that caricature was the
tribute that mediocrity paid to genius. As to genius, on
his entry into the United States, Wilde had admitted shyly
to the U.S. Customs that it was all he had to declare. Not
since the noble savage had been brought to England in
the eighteenth century had there been such curiosity
about a new human specimen as there was about Wilde.

Although Wilde was to say later that America and
England had everything in common except language and
manners, his opening lecture at Chickering Hall in New
York was complimentary to the United States and archly
derogatory of England. Wilde found, he said to his audience, "something Hellenic in your air and world," and
something of the "quicker breath of the joy and power of
Elizabethan England." He noted that the "Renaissance"
of art which he was heralding "must be completed in the
U.S." A little irritated by the heavy ridicule of his movement in the mother country, Wilde observed: "To know
nothing about their great men is one of the necessary elements of English education." He cheerfully accepted as
his emblems those assigned him by the journalists—the
sunflower and the lily. He praised them as perfect models

of design. The main portion of his manifesto or lecture
turned upon the message of beauty. Wilde spoke in somewhat exalted and visionary terms of that "Hellenism"
which had "filled some of us, at least, with the lofty and
passionate ambition to go forth into far and fair lands
with some message for the nations and some mission for
the world . . ." He announced that art carried no formula
of morality, no neat set of philosophical truths, no system
of life and conduct, but that it existed only to delight.
Poems were not moral or immoral, but merely well or
badly written. The test of any civilization was whether it
admired and created beauty, a thesis which was original
with Ruskin. He went on to note that "national hatreds
are always strongest where culture is lowest." Somewhat
later in life he voiced the hope that international peace
might be based upon aesthetics; that statesmen would
say: "We will not go to war with France—because her
prose is perfect." He was careful, after high tribute, to
purge Ruskin, whom he regarded as the right-wing leader
of the Aesthetic school in England: ". . . in his art criticism . . . his whole method of approaching art, we are no
longer with him; for the keynote to his aesthetic system
is ethical always. He would judge of a picture by the
amount of noble moral ideas it expresses; but to us . . .
the rule of art is not the rule of morals . . ." Beauty was
its own justification and more; ". . . the secret of life is in
art," were his concluding words.

Wilde evoked favorable publicity, and as a result of his
four-score lectures delivered throughout America and
Canada, he was in demand for a round-the-country lecture tour on his return to England; "Personal Impressions
of America" was his topic.

While he was on tour, Wilde's comments on American
life kept him in the news. Much as he disliked the noise
and bustle of a country where the nightingale had been
displaced by the steam whistle, and everyone seemed
hurrying to catch a train, the presence of the dynamo
seemed not to displease him. On shipboard on the way
across he had written a poem about the engine room

where "leap the long rods of polished steel." He observed of Chicago, Sandburg's city of the big shoulders: "I have always wished to believe that the line of strength and the line of beauty are one. That wish was realized when I contemplated American machinery. . . . the water-works at Chicago . . . the rise and fall of the steel rods, the symmetrical motion of the great wheels is the most beautifully rhythmic thing I have ever seen." O'Neill's Hairy Ape could not have put it better.

A few of his quips are perhaps worth preserving; his comment on polygamy while visiting the Mormon settlement in Salt Lake City: "How much more poetic it is to marry one and love many." He joked about Southern patriotism, noting that he could hardly admire a beautiful moon without the reminder: "But you should have seen it before the war." His comment on Niagara Falls, honeymoon center of America in his day, was: "the stupendous waterfall must be one of the earliest, if not the keenest, disappointments in American married life." He dismissed American novels as "American dry goods," but praised American girls as "little oases of pretty unreasonableness in a vast desert of common sense." The Western miners he felt to be the best dressed men in America, comparing them with the seventeenth-century Cavaliers. China Town in San Francisco was our most artistic city where "rough melancholy Oriental workmen" took "tea out of china cups as delicate as the petals of a rose-leaf" and restaurant bills were presented on rice paper marked with India ink so that they "looked like birds etched on a fan."

Contemporary descriptions of him both in America and England give a vivid notion of the impression made by the apostle of aestheticism. In the American *Lady's Pictorial,* we have an interesting record (presumably written by a lady admirer), who found him in his hotel in an over-heated room, seated before the fire-place on "an immense wolf-rug, bordered with scarlet." In manner he was the true aesthete, ". . . wearied . . . In a languid, half enervated manner he gently sipped hot chocolate . . . inhaled a long, deep whiff . . . from a cigarette held lightly in his white and shapely hand." It was in the "at home" manner of Algernon and Jack of *The Importance of Being Earnest*. So was the apparel; he wore a "smoking suit of dark brown velvet faced with lapels of red quilted silk. The ends of a long dark necktie floated on the facing like seaweed on foam tinged by the dying sun . . . patent leather shoes with light cloth uppers." The reporter continues, noting that his trousers (the genteel writer calls them his "nether garments") had "red stripes . . . Only in the evening was he wont to don knee-breeches." As for Wilde's physical personality, she notes: "Long masses of dark, brown hair fell in odd curves of beauty over his broad shoulders . . . The full, rather sensuous lips showed to perfection the nobility of his countenance . . . A Grecian nose and a well-tinged flush of health on the poet's face . . . a truly remarkable one. The eyes were large, dark and ever-changing in expression." After noting his "white walking stick" the writer concludes ". . . always a man, and always a perfect gentleman."

Richard LeGallienne in his book *The Romantic '90's* has likewise left us a picture of Wilde, observed just a few months later when Wilde had returned to England to continue his lectures; the male version, although LeGallienne was an admirer of Wilde, is a trifle less admiring: "At that time Wilde had abandoned his knee-breeches and was dressed in a sort of Georgian costume, with tight pantaloon trousers . . . His amber-coloured hair . . . unashamedly curled and massively modelled to his head . . . large figure . . . big loose face, grossly jawed with thick, sensuous lips, and a certain fat effeminacy about him, suggested a sort of caricatured Dionysius disguised as a rather heavy dandy of the Regency period . . ." LeGallienne emphasized what Shaw insisted upon as in part the basis of Wilde's homosexuality, a bodily abnormality verging on giantism, something (continuing LeGallienne's description): "grotesquely excessive about his whole appearance and while he was in a way handsome, [he was like an] enormous doll, a preposterous exaggerated puppet such as smile foolishly from floats at the Nice carnival. But his strong, humorous haughty eyes, his good brow and fine nose . . . his superb and rather insolent aplomb . . . And, of course, his wonderful golden voice, . . . modulated with elaborate self-consciousness. Exotic . . . entirely different from the dilettante, lily-like 'aesthete' . . . impudent humour and sound common sense . . . this friend of dreaming and rebellious youth . . ."

These two descriptions indicate sharply the difference between a mere catalogue of personal traits and facts, and a portrait of the aesthete as a young man. Wilde was simultaneously something monstrous and glamorous to the young men of his time, "this friend of dreaming and rebellious youth." His glamour appealed to their idealizing impulse and his exotic grotesqueness to their rebelliousness. Such then was Wilde, the travelling exhibit of dandyism and aestheticism. Wilde wore the uniform of a dandyism that was of the mind as well as of the person. Mental dandyism exalts style and form, and manifests itself in paradox and epigram: *The Importance of Being Earnest* is conceived in the form of paradox, a transvaluation in which the trivial is taken seriously and the serious lightly. The individual statements in the play are in the form of the epigram, which in Wilde's hands was (like the epitaph) a brief statement of half truths, but (contrary to the epitaph) was expressed in a provocative and explosive manner. The fraction of the truth thus obtruded was the least palatable and the most shocking to Victorian smugness.

Actually Wilde's conception of the dandy, as seen from without, was more studiously restrained in his dramatic presentations than in his own person. Lord Goring, for example, in *An Ideal Husband* represents the dress of the dandy: "Enter Lord Goring in evening dress with a buttonhole. He is wearing a silk hat and Inverness cape. White-gloved, he carries a Louis Seize cane. His are all the delicate fopperies of Fashion." The personal attendants of the dandy are equally distinctive: Phipps, for example, "is a mask with a manner. Of his intellectual or emotional life, history knows nothing. He represents the dominance of form." Such are Wilde's stage directions. The more intimate spirit and style of the dandy are also mirrored in Lord Goring: "A well-bred expressionless face. He is clever, but would not like to be thought so. A flawless dandy, he would be annoyed if he were considered romantic. He plays with life, and is on perfectly good terms with the world." His motto: "To love oneself is the beginning of a life-long romance." What critics have said of literary expression is emphatically true of the entire existence of the dandy: "The style is the man."

The mind of the dandy is adequately displayed in Wilde's play *A Woman of No Importance;* there is a dialogue between the worldly dandy Lord Illingworth and the simple artless young man Gerald Arbuthnot. Lord Illingworth says, "A man who can dominate a London dinner-table can dominate the world. The future belongs to the dandy. It is the exquisites who are going to rule . . . A well-tied tie is the first serious step in life." Such was the easy twilight mood of Victorian civilization before its limbs had been fractured by two world wars. Young Gerald presents a series of questions which are like a series of fine china dishes held in the hand successively; the silk-hatted, opera-cloaked man with the flashing silver pistol shivers each into delicate fragments:

GERALD: Still there are many different kinds of women, aren't there?

LORD ILLINGWORTH: Only two kinds in society; the plain and the coloured.

GERALD: But there are good women in society, aren't there?

LORD ILLINGWORTH: Far too many.

GERALD: But do you think women shouldn't be good?

LORD ILLINGWORTH: One should never tell them so, they'd all become good at once.

GERALD: You have never been married, Lord Illingworth, have you?

LORD ILLINGWORTH: Men marry because they are tired; women because they are curious. Both are disappointed.

GERALD: But don't you think one can be happy when one is married?

LORD ILLINGWORTH: Perfectly happy. But the happiness of

a married man, my dear Gerald, depends on the people he has not married.

GERALD: But if one is in love?

LORD ILLINGWORTH: One should always be in love. That is the reason one should never marry.

GERALD: Love is a very wonderful thing, isn't it?

LORD ILLINGWORTH: When one is in love one begins by deceiving oneself. And one ends by deceiving others. That is what the world calls a romance. But a really *grande passion* is comparatively rare nowadays. It is the privilege of people who have nothing to do.

Wilde's practical application to life and human relations of Pater's aestheticism was a search for sensational statement and pleasure that tended to separate not only husband from wife, but child from parent: "Children begin by loving their parents. After a time they judge them. Rarely if ever do they forgive them." The critical aestheticism of the dandy separated art from life, imagination from experience, led to a preference of mannerism to style, surface virtuosity and witty triviality to insight and feeling. Hence in all of Wilde's comedies, statement and character have frequently very little to do with one another. Witty characters from different plays could be interchanged; witticisms within a given play could be assigned arbitrarily to other characters without loss of consistency. Moreover, in all of the comedies except *The Importance of Being Earnest* Wilde has tried to mix the water of a too-easy sentimentalism and the oil of a glossy cynicism. A few of the propositions of his artistic credo illustrate the working of his mind: "To introduce real people into a novel or a play is a sign of an unimaginative mind . . . The colours of a flower may suggest to one the plot of a tragedy . . . Everything in art matters except the subject . . . The first duty in life is to be as artificial as possible . . . In all important matters, style, not sincerity, is the essential . . . There are no real emotions left —only extraordinary adjectives." It was this very separation of living and feeling that isolated Wilde from his perity, intoxicated with success, Wilde became presumptuous and arrogant, driven seemingly by a reckless self-will into a collision with the powers that were to crush him. "Blindly I staggered as an ox to the shambles," he declared later; "I had made a gigantic psychological error." His error was, in essence, that of bringing himself into the court of public opinion with the belief that he could dominate juries as he had dominated theatre audiences and dinner parties. Wilde later referred to his tragedy as one "lacking in style," a catastrophe based on a combination of "absolute idiocy with vulgar bravado." A repulsive route for the decline and fall of a dandy. Perhaps the art that Wilde's life most closely imitated was that of Flaubert, one of the French writers who so fascinated Wilde, although Wilde, intent upon Flaubert's style, obviously missed the moral. For Flaubert's *Emma Bovary* is a ruthless autopsy of romanticism, a morbid study of the romantic pursuit of exotic, voluptuous pleasure. Flaubert presented the romantic attempt to escape the humdrum of life as a pathological infection of the imagination, a disease leading feverishly to an abject and gruesome ending. Wilde's decline illustrated Flaubert's Bovaryism in a luxurious interlude of sexual inversion. "He has been mad for the last three years," exclaimed his wife Constance at the time of the trial. Mad after the manner of Emma Bovary in the pursuit of a voluptuous illusion, one which Wilde has himself described somewhat after the manner of the romantic clown who writes with a broken heart. His record of his madness is given in his *Epistola: in Carcere et Vinculis,* now known after the title given it by a friend of Wilde's as *De Profundis.*

In one of his plays Wilde had a character say of marriage and its break-up: "The Book of Life begins with a man and a woman in a garden. It ends with Revelations." Wilde's own marriage strangely paralleled his Biblical whimsy. At the time of his marriage, he dedicated to his wife Constance one of the editions of his *Poems*. In the dedicatory poem, he conceived of his verses under the figure of petals of flowers:

friends and eventually brought him into a fatal colli
with the law.

Although Wilde's successful cultivation of notoriet
the end of the '70's and during the early '80's made
name—if not a household—then a salon word, it did
at once inspire him to literary creation. He was simply
engaged in acting the role of the dandy that he had not y
found a literary expression for it. Soon after his successi
tours he married Constance Lloyd, possessor of a mode
fortune, and moved to a more respectable London res
dence. He settled into domestic life, had two childrei
and edited women's fashion magazines to which he con
tributed literary notes and book reviews. His elaborate
and "chic" descriptions of the costume of his female characters in his later stage directions reveal this connection.
He was later connected with the *Pall Mall Gazette*. During the second half of the decade, Wilde came more and
more under the spell of French writers, such as Baudelaire, Flaubert, Huysmans, writers of the "decadent"
school. His poem *The Sphinx,* his play *Salomé,* and his
short novel *The Picture of Dorian Gray* clearly reflect
these influences. The latter work elicited such epithets
from reviewers as "poisonous," "leprous," "degenerate";
such insinuations of secret and criminal vice, of unfeeling
cruelty, of a heartless hedonism were later brought to
bear against Wilde during his trial. Then quite suddenly
in the early years of the '90's Wilde's genius leaped up-
wards like a silvery fountain; within a very few years he
had presented four plays in London's West End, two of
them playing simultaneously, the culminating work being
*The Importance of Being Earnest. Lady Windermere's
Fan* appeared in 1892, *A Woman of No Importance* in
1893, and in 1895, in January, *An Ideal Husband* was
delighting audiences. *The Importance of Being Earnest,*
an even more dazzling success, appeared a month later.

It was one of Wilde's favorite maxims that life imitated art. Ironically his own life did just that. At the pin-
nacle of his popularity and prosperity, his own conduct
was a tragic dramatization of hybris. Coarsened by pros-

For if of these fallen petals
   One to you seem fair
Love will waft it till it settle
   On your hair.

And when wind and winter harden
   All the lovely land
It will whisper of the garden
   You will understand.

If that sentiment pointed to the man and the woman and the "garden," the Old Bailey criminal court was the book of Revelations; the findings of the court were such that "all the lovely land" was hardened, and Constance did not, would not—perhaps could not—understand.

Indeed it was most difficult for Victorians generally to understand, for they were confronted with a scandalous trial turning upon the disclosures of Wilde's bi-sexual nature. *Bi-sexual* would seem to be the correct term. At the time of his marriage to Constance Lloyd in 1884, a union issuing in the birth of two children, Cyril born in 1885 and Vyvyan in 1886, Wilde was apparently leading a normal domestic existence. He evidently became involved in pederasty in the late '80's and successfully concealed it even from his close friends. Shaw, upon hearing the facts, was astonished.

By 1891, beginning with the publication of *The Picture of Dorian Gray,* ugly rumours had been set afloat. The novel had insinuated the theme of homosexual indulgence in remote, sordid, waterfront hideaways. Later his poem *The Sphinx,* with its deliberate artificial, metallic decadence further suggested hankering for grotesque, monstrous vice. Indeed from the beginning of his advocacy of art for art's sake, Wilde had invited the suspicions of the Victorian fathers. Their severe disapproval of the pursuit of pleasure led them to assume that young men who begin burning with hard, gem-like flames would eventually—to put it vulgarly—burn for hard, gem-liking dames. But hostile critics had not dared even to imagine sexual divagation turning into actual sexual deviation. In fact one of the notable features of the trial was the shocked horror with which many learned of this hidden dimension of the sexual life. When headlines reported that Wilde, the arch transgressor, was seen reading a yellow book, angry citizens proceeded to stone the windows of the offices of *The Yellow Book,* an *avante garde* publication of the time. Actually Wilde's yellow book, *a* yellow book, was a French publication having nothing to do with the magazine. It was *Aphrodite* by Pierre Louys. Yellow was the "theme" color of the '90's, symbolizing the bizarre and the modern.

The train of events which were to issue in Wilde's imprisonment for two years at hard labor was set in motion when the poet Lionel Johnson introduced Wilde to Lord Douglas—young, handsome, and aristocratic, pert and pampered. The young man with the splendidly ancient name was irresistible to the now somewhat corpulent dandy, who had proclaimed, "I can resist anything but temptation." Wilde's dramatic successes supplied him with the abundant income which enabled him to entertain in a theatrically flashy manner—elaborate dinners, luxurious supper-parties with expensive favors at the Café Royal, extravagant hotel accommodations for himself and friends. In the company of Lord Douglas (whom many thought to be and Shaw called "that horrid little brat"), Wilde made flash visits to Cairo and Paris in search of exotic and voluptuous adventure. The two friends became central figures, scarcely veiled, in a scandalous novel of 1894, *The Green Carnation,* written by Robert Hichens. As Wilde's favorite buttonhole, almost his signature-flower, was a green carnation, there could be little doubt as to the reference. As the rumors spread and the whisperings grew darker, Wilde became only more reckless. For those of Arnold's generation who felt that the study of the classics helped people to see life steadily and to see it whole, Wilde, the proficient Greek student, was the embarrassment of the century.

The crucial figure in the tragedy which overtook Wilde was the father of Lord Douglas, the Marquess of Queensbury. He was a man of violent, epileptic temper and of headlong disposition, a kind of titled Squire Western on the loose in London, determined to separate his son from the company of Wilde. He can scarcely be thought of as a fatherly heart, tenderly yearning to reclaim an erring son from profligate companions. His personal biography precludes any imputation of high-minded concern. Illustrative of his tempestuous nature was his appearance, or attempted appearance, at the opening night of *The Importance of Being Earnest* armed with a bouquet of turnips and parsnips which he intended to hurl at the author of the play on his being summoned to the stage. Only a police cordon prevented his entry to the theatre. The "screaming, scarlet Marquis" was Wilde's description of him. But the Marquess, barbarian or not, succeeded in dragging into the light a screaming scarlet scandal which lodged Wilde in jail from May of 1895 to May of 1897. For all of his obtuseness and violence, in his game with Wilde, the Marquess played the winning card. He played it quite literally; for the match that kindled the explosions was a card which he left for Wilde at the latter's club— the Albermarle. On it the Marquess had insultingly inscribed "somdomite"—an improper word, improperly spelled. Wilde decided to sue the Marquess for libel. At a meeting at the Café Royal, two of Wilde's friends attempted strenuously to dissuade him from such a course. Bernard Shaw and Frank Harris warned him against his intended course of action: Harris, in particular, advised him to write a letter to *The Times,* disavowing the imputed vice, pointing out that the Marquess was too subhuman to profit from legal chastisement. Then, continued Harris, Wilde was to leave on a trip to Paris, conspicuously accompanied by his wife. Also present at the meeting was young Douglas. He was desperately eager to get his father into court in order to expose, punish, and humiliate him. He was petulantly willing to risk Wilde's career in order to have a shot at the hated parent. Wilde, perversely dominated by young Lord Douglas, prosecuted the Marquess. But the latter had prepared his defense too carefully; he had acquired or bought too many witnesses to Wilde's sexual deviations. Wilde belatedly withdrew his action. But now the State intervened and successfully turned the prosecution against Wilde in criminal court.

In an interval between a jury-disagreement and a re-trial, Wilde was out on bail. Again his friends urged him to escape to the Continent and take refuge there, conjecturing that Wilde would certainly lose his case. Stubbornly, with a kind of benumbed obstinacy, Wilde again refused advice. His motives were a mixture of pride, fatalism, and arrogance. He felt that he could not, with honor, run away; perhaps he felt that he could by clever repartee talk his way out of the prosecution; to some friends he appeared to have the feeling that the matter was in the hands of an overruling fate, that he was but an actor in a drama. Both sentiment and skill were against Wilde. Ostensibly a father was attempting to rescue his son from a fate "worse than death." Wilde's legal counsel was inept and incompetent. In the collapse of his defense, Wilde's talent, his health, and life were also involved. He never recovered from the disaster.

Of his history after judgment was passed against him, there is little to be said. During his imprisonment, Lugné-Poë produced his *Salomé,* a Biblical drama, at the Theatre de L'Oeuvre in Paris. The prison experience resulted in some letters to newspapers on the deplorable conduct of the jails. After his release, Wilde wrote *The Ballad of Reading Gaol,* turning on the execution by hanging of a guardsman who had murdered his wife. In melody and form it is clearly a reminiscence of Coleridge's *Ancient Mariner.* Actually, serious emotions—melodrama, pathos, the tragic infirmity of man—were beyond Wilde's reach. His gift was to amuse, divert, startle, but not to rise to a plane of tragic dignity. Consequently the poem rings true only at those rare moments in which there is an opening for satiric irony, such as the cruelly impersonal nature of legal retribution, the absence of any consolation or reprieve for the prisoner doomed to swing for the gallows:

The Governor was strong upon
The Regulations Act;
The Doctor said that Death was but
A scientific fact:
And twice a day the Chaplain called,
And left a little tract.

Wilde also felt impelled to write a sort of spiritual auto-biography, now known as the *De Profundis.*

Wilde's remaining years were spent on the Continent, mainly in France. He assumed the name of Sebastian Melmoth; the first name suggested the suffering martyr. *Melmoth the Wanderer* was the title of a gothic novel by Charles Maturin, a distant relative of Wilde's. His mother was Maturin's grand-niece; as Byron was also a friend of Maturin, we are provided with another curious link with Byron. It is far too easy to sketch Wilde's few declining years in a mood of melodramatic pathos; indeed Wilde's last days remind one of those of another dandy, Beau Brummel, insofar as a seedy and sad ending contrasts with former days of brilliant success. Wilde, the delightful Playboy of the West End World of London, finished his journey in Paris; he died in a hotel room located in a street called, appropriately enough, the Rue des Beaux Arts. The date was 30 November 1900. Wilde was received into the Roman Catholic Church before his death by an English Passionist father. Wilde's speech was paralyzed, but he was conscious. At the end he was in great pain and delirium, despite repeated injections of morphine. The cause of his death was cerebral meningitis.

Wilde is still a highly controversial figure, evaluations both of his works and his character clashing sharply. Along with Byron, Shaw, and Shakespeare, he is one of the most widely translated English writers. His European reputation is perhaps higher than his native one. One issue is placed quite beyond dispute, agreed upon by both moralists and literary critics: *The Importance of Being Earnest* is a fountain of unfailing delight.

THE PLAY

"Oh, Oscar! You cannot surely be in earnest. You can only be joking." (Constance Wilde to her husband Oscar)

The quoted words of wifely perplexity followed upon Wilde's facetious declaration that Divine Providence protected the heathen cannibal against starvation by opportunely sending him nice plump missionaries. Mrs. Wilde, pretty and domestic, evangelically serious, and ardent supporter of the Church Foreign Missions Society, often was troubled by her hubsand's whimsicalities. Readers should not approach the play in her spirit. We must not worry overmuch upon what peg to hang it: whether that of broad farce, comedy of manners, a specimen of the "well-made" play. It touches upon all of these and is none of them. Perhaps *The Importance of Being Earnest* is best regarded as a unique specimen of the comedy of cleverness, standing between Sheridan's comedy of manners and Shaw's comedy of ideas. As Wilde developed his dramatic talent, he more and more dramatized his own conversational cleverness. He accused Whistler, the noted wit and painter, of spelling Art with a capital "I." But critics have before now observed of Wilde's literary progress that his characters became *de plus en plus Oscarisé*. Generally a novel or play of Wilde's contains a character especially representative of its creator's temperament and views, such as Lord Henry in *The Picture of Dorian Gray,* Cecil Graham in *Lady Windermere's Fan,* Lord Illingworth in *A Woman of No Importance,* Lord Goring in *An Ideal Husband.* They are all the type of the suave, supercilious dandy. But in *The Importance of Being Earnest,* despite the variety of roles, the voice of the characters is that of Oscar. The play is almost entirely *Oscarisé.*

Like his own personality the play is a blend of anti-thetical elements. Wilde's personal manner was to deliver facetious, paradoxical, or trivial declarations in a spirit of formal, measured gravity—being neither too pontifical or affectedly pompous, nor yet too archly or consciously cute and comic. The lines of the play must be delivered in that way. In the composite texture of the play we have brilliant, copious, elaborately sophisticated dialogue whose tone is one of elegant flippancy and restrained mock-seriousness. This highly self-conscious verbal wit rests upon a plot that is broadly farcical, boisterously improbable—something that might have been the production of Tony Lumpkin, the practical joker and inventive prankster in Goldsmith's *She Stoops to Conquer*. The play as a whole is a blending of the high-comedy spirit of Congreve or Sheridan with the farcical spirit of the Marx Brothers. Yet there is an element of continuity between the dialogue and the plot, that of cleverly contrived nonsense. In the dialogue, conventional thought—and in the plot, conventional conduct—are equally turned topsy-turvy. The characters do not say what they think; what they say has little connection with what they do. Jack and Algernon, posing as cynical bachelor dandies, discreetly allude to surreptitiously irregular lives, yet there are no facts to convict them of anything unvirtuous; they deplore the doldrums of marriage and domesticity even as they cheerfully become engaged. The Rev. Chasuble exalts the celibacy of the Primitive Church even as he is entering the marital sanctuary of the primitive urges. The articulate Miss Prism, a pillar of propriety, is actually more rejoiced at the recovery of her handbag than at the restoration of the child whose infancy she had abandoned to a railway terminal cloakroom.

Despite the essentially artificial world of the play, there are elements of realistic satire. The Bunburying bachelors, for example, constitute a playful satire on the Victorian double-standard. The Rev. Chasuble is a light thrust at the High Church movement within the Established Church and its pre-occupation with a restoration of primitive church practices, its reintroduction of vestments, etc. His name is suggestive òf the latter, the chasuble being an ecclesiastical vestment. Lady Bracknell is a caricature of the Victorian *grande dame* in her plenipotentiary and peremptory manner; she is repeated with variations in Shaw's *Major Barbara* in the person of Lady Britomart (the trick ending in Shaw's play turning upon a sudden disclosure concerning birth is also reminiscent of Wilde's comedy).

In both plot and dialogue there are also elements of satire; satirically, however, these elements are not related —and this may be a weakness in the construction of the play. The object of the satire of the plot has little or nothing to do with that of the dialogue. The plot is a pleasant parody of plots (of the type of Fielding's *Tom Jones*) which turn upon the dramatic discovery of the long-lost heir, the sudden restoration of the long-lost brother. Moreover, the long leg of coincidence upon which such plots uncertainly balance is pulled remorselessly in the situation of the absentminded interchange of the manuscript of a novel and a baby on the part of a maid who afterwards quite unknowingly becomes part of the domestic establishment of the lost baby—now grown to manhood. A further satiric ingredient of the plot is its parody of the traditional obstacle that stands between the union of loving souls: primarily—the imperious necessity of two young men possessing the given name of Ernest before they can be accepted as husbands. A secondary obstacle to union is parodied in the class-barrier, represented by the firm-minded Lady Bracknell, who refuses to allow "our only daughter—a girl brought up with the utmost care—to marry into a cloak-room, and form an alliance with a parcel." Simultaneously parodied is the reverse side of this conventional obstacle of romantic fiction, the psychology whereby the óbstacle intensifies the love of the young people and fortifies their loyalty: "The story of your romantic origin, as related to me by mamma, with unpleasing comments, has naturally stirred the deeper fibers of my nature . . . The simplicity of your character makes you exquisitely incomprehensible to me." The farcical convention of mistaken identity is amusingly played with in the confusion existing between Gwendolen and Cecily as to who possesses the mythical "Ernest," and in Miss Prism's being mistaken by Jack for his mother in the disclosure scene. Love-at-first-sight is lightly mocked at in the scene in which the contents of Cecily's diary are revealed to Algernon; romantically heroic sacrifice of lover for lady is parodied in the scene in which the gentlemen announce their reckless readiness to undergo baptism, the ladies alternately exclaiming: ". . . you are prepared to do this terrible thing . . . To please me you are ready to face this fearful ordeal?" Indeed, deliberately or by inadvertence Wilde's plot parodies itself, for at the end the author fails to supply Algernon with the name of Ernest, despite the fact that Cecily has not waived her insistence on this point; moreover Wilde makes no comment on the fact that "Jack" as Ernest is to marry his own first-cousin.

In a larger sense, Wilde handles the plot so as to make it a parody of conventional dramatic farce; it is a mock-drama in something of the sense in which that other finely wrought triviality, Pope's *Rape of the Lock,* is a mock-epic. In *The Importance of Being Earnest* the characters do not react to events as they do in ordinary farce; their behavior is the conventional behavior inverted: they respond flippantly to the solemn and with mock-solemnity to the trivial. Traditionally the dramatic justification for farcical construction is that the extraordinary circumstances dominating the characters provoke from them emotionally intense responses. Such was the spirit of Congreve, Goldsmith, and Sheridan in the handling of farcical situations in *The Way of the World, She Stoops to Conquer, The Rivals,* and *The School for Scandal:* Young Marlowe writhes in acute embarrassment in discovering the mistakes of the evening; old Mr. Hardcastle vibrates with indignation when victimized by those mistakes; Lady Wishfort, Old Mrs. Hardcastle, Lydia Languish storm violently at the deceptions and impostures to

which they are subjected; the direction of life of Lady
Teazle is altered on the throwing down of the screen;
Joseph Surface squirms with explanatory and apologetic
device. But in Wilde's plot, the characters are not im-
mersed in the action; they transcend the action and stand
outside of history, as it were. Regardless of the crucial
implications of their situation, they respond with studied
self-possession, with bland detachment, or nonchalant
brightness.

Illustrations of the foregoing will occur to any reader.
Dr. Chasuble on hearing that Jack's brother has died in
Paris of a chill has not more than concluded his warm
condolences (adding a clinical footnote: "I myself am
peculiarly susceptible to draughts,") than Algernon's
sudden arrival and impersonation of the fictional brother
upsets the report; his miraculous restoration to life is
thereupon greeted by Dr. Chasuble with congratulatory
blandness: "These are very joyful tidings." In the revelation scene in which Jack Worthing's true identity is
dramatically disclosed by the evidence of the handbag,
Miss Prism's outrageous negligence in having originally
mislaid the baby generates no remorse. She is more interested in the recovery of lost property than in the restoration of the lost child; instead of anguished confession of
error and astonishment at the circumstances that had
brought the truth to light, she says in grey neutrality of
voice: "The bag is undoubtedly mine. I am delighted to
have it so unexpectedly restored to me. It has been a
great inconvenience being without it all these years." And
in what should have been the nervously tremulous moment of identifying the bag, Miss Prism examines the decisive markings—a stain and her initials—and reports
on them with exquisitely gratuitous irrelevance: the
stain "caused by the explosion of a temperance beverage,"
and the initials remarkable for having been purchased
"in an extravagant mood." Once the bag has been iden-
tified, Jack, upon whose origins the news sheds such
dazzling light, turns to Lady Bracknell who can with this
clue inform him of his real parentage. His approach to

the oracle is politely languorous: "Lady Bracknell, I hate to seem inquisitive . . ." Then on discovery that his name is really Ernest, he confesses, ". . . it is a terrible thing for a man to find out suddenly that all his life he has been speaking nothing but the truth. Can you forgive me?"

In his characterization, where emotion is usually displayed, Wilde underplays it, as the instances just cited indicate, or reverses it. For example, one expects some delicacy of compassion for the condition of poor Bunbury. But Lady Bracknell exclaims: ". . . I think it is high time that Mr. Bunbury made up his mind whether he is going to live or to die. This shilly-shallying with the question is absurd." Similarly, to Jack's wistful confession that he has lost both parents, Lady Bracknell responds: "To lose one parent, Mr. Worthing, may be regarded as a misfortune; to lose both looks like carelessness." Although human infirmity and misfortune fail to move her, Lady Bracknell replies enthusiastically to Jack's confession that he smokes: "I am glad to hear it. A man should always have an occupation of some kind. There are far too many idle men in London as it is." Miss Prism, too, reacts to the trivial with mock-gravity: she admonishes her charge Cecily to omit "The chapter on the Fall of the Rupee . . . It is somewhat too sensational. Even these metallic problems have their melodramatic side." But on the contrary, when Miss Prism is confronted with the sad announcement of the death of the brother of her employer, she remarks with casual off-handedness, "What a lesson for him! I trust he will profit by it."

There is still another reversal of conventional construction in the characterization of Dr. Chasuble and Miss Prism. Traditionally the middle-aged couple, or the elderly bachelor or spinster, or the elderly seekers of love are made game of. They take part in the comedy as a foil and off-set to the gay, young, witty couples. In Wilde's play there are no Lady Wishforts, no Mrs. Malaprops, no Sir Peter Teazles to be made ludicrous or deceived or revealed as obtuse. Chasuble and Prism are pitched in mood and key much as are the other characters. Miss

Prism may in name be a telescoping of "prim" and "prissy"—the traits of the Victorian spinster. Still, she is as pert and saucy as the others; on the reversal of the news of brother "Ernest's" death, she says: "After we had all been resigned to his loss, his sudden return seems to me peculiarly distressing." As the pursuing woman, she manifests none of the shy retirement expected of the Victorian female. Dr. Chasuble's reverence for the celibate life, he confides, is owing to the fact that "the precept as well as the practice of the Primitive Church was distinctly against matrimony." To this the purposeful Miss Prism replies tartly: "That is obviously the reason why the Primitive Church has not lasted up to the present day." Finally, the dowager Lady Bracknell, although an exaggerated, is likewise a commanding and imposing presence.

A final departure from conventional construction in the play is the omission of the slow-witted or the awkward or the pretentious or affected clown or buffoon. There are no Bob Acres, no Petulants or Witwouds, no Sir Benjamin Backbites in the play. There is within the framework of the play no specific chopping block against which the witty satiric speeches of the play may direct themselves. But the clown or fool is there by implication. It is the scheme of Victorian values for which there is no concrete representative in the play as, for instance, there is in Ibsen's *Ghosts, Enemy of the People,* etc. And this brings us back to our original observation that the satire of the dialogue has little to do with the parody of the plot. The former is directed for the most part against the values that were revered by the eminent pillars of Victorian society.

In title and texture, *The Importance of Being Earnest* is a playful satire on the old-fashioned, mid-Victorian character already obsolescent by Wilde's time. The good man of the pre-revolutionary eighteenth century, such as Squire Allworthy of Fielding's *Tom Jones,* approved of what was virtuous, honorable, and able. The good man of the mid-Victorian period, as presented in Tennyson's *Idylls of the King* and elsewhere, was noble, manly, and pure. (In our time, the good "personality" is normal, healthy, and adjusted.) The eighteenth-century man's virtue had nothing mystical about it; it called for fulfilling one's duty to family, friends, and neighbors. His honor was simply that code of conduct prescribed by his class. (The twentieth-century man aims at being just like everyone else—only more so?) But the ideal mid-Victorian character embodied aspirations towards a superior inner fineness of feeling, a purity of motive, a loftiness of aim, an elevation of mind. As extremes of contrast, one thinks of the Victorian gentleman as defined by Cardinal Newman in *The Idea of a University* and the eighteenth-century gentleman as represented by Lord Chesterfield and his Letters. To recur to our other references, Tennyson's Sir Galahad would be quite puzzling to Fielding's Squire Allworthy; Allworthy might promise Tom Jones the strength of one if Tom's heart was kindly and his head quite clear; Sir Galahad had the strength of ten—moral as well as physical, hence nobility united to manliness—because his heart was pure. But between Fielding and Chesterfield, on the one hand, and Tennyson and Newman, on the other, flow the great currents of the romantic movement with its tumultuous aspirations towards a more ideal type of humanity. The chief outward sign of this Victorian ideal man was his earnestness. In a letter of 1881, Matthew Arnold, one of the minor prophets of the Victorian period, said of Carlyle, one of the major prophets: "He was always 'carrying coals to Newcastle,' . . . preaching earnestness to a nation that had it by nature, but was less abundantly supplied with other things." The preoccupation with it was excessive because to the Victorian earnestness was a quasi-sacramental trait —an outward sign or manifestation of the inward graces of nobility, purity, manliness of character. Its opposite, the sure index to a subtle inner corruption, was a habitual flippancy of tone and frivolity of attitude. In 1851, Ruskin, another leading Victorian prophet and teacher, in his discussion of the new pre-Raphaelite movement in art, observed, "We are intended, as long as we live, to be in a state of intense moral effort . . . Our energies are to be given to the soul's work—to the great fight with the Dragon . . ." Ruskin was especially severe towards artists who "are expected, and themselves expect, to make their bread *by being clever*— . . . and are . . . for the most part, trying to be clever, and so living in an utterly false state of mind and action." Wilde's play from its title to its last line ("I've now realized for the first time in my life the Importance of Being Earnest.") is an unabashedly clever, an ironically flippant, and a gaily frivolous burlesque of this Victorian life-attitude. The earnest old prophets are gently nudged aside in favor of London's Playboys of the West End World. Hence Jack weary of being a pillar of society—a guardian—invents a brother Ernest as a relief from having "to adopt a high moral tone on all subjects."

In one way and another, most of the personal, domestic, and social sanctities of the Victorians are subjected to Wilde's light bantering satire. For example, no institution was more exalted in mind by the Victorian than the family; the fireside was his altar; to question the values of family life was to stand before the temple and scoff. Wilde was at it constantly. The impeccable servant Lane defines marriage as "a misunderstanding between myself and a young person." He apologizes for having introduced the topic of family life into conversation: ". . . not a very interesting subject. I never think of it myself." The Bunbury ruse exists because "in married life three is company and two is none." Algernon asserts that "divorces are made in heaven;" widows are described as looking "quite twenty years younger" and having their "hair . . . turned quite gold from grief."

Another of the obvious Victorian preoccupations was that of reform and improvement, social and personal. The ubiquitous Victorian diary, for example, was a record to be used for self-examination with a view to ascertaining one's backslidings and advancements. Wilde refers to it merely as a record of purple passages meant for publication. Cecily remarks that her diary is "simply a very young girl's record of her own thoughts and impressions, and consequently meant for publication." Gwendolen says of her diary: "I never travel without my diary. One should always have something sensational to read on the train."

The great Victorian invention, the social conscience, is treated lightly. Miss Prism observes: "I am not in favour of this modern mania for turning bad people into good people at a moment's notice." Perverse mention is made of a "Society for Preventing Discontent among the Upper Orders." Lady Bracknell, misunderstanding a report that Bunbury had been "exploded," exclaims, "I was not aware that Mr. Bunbury was interested in social legislation. If so, he is well punished for his morbidity."

Victorian social standards demanded of the proper female that she acquire refinement and respectability. Lady Bracknell, seeking a clue to the identification of the Miss Prism mentioned in her presence, asks whether she is a "female of repellent aspect." On being admonished that Miss Prism is "the most cultivated of ladies, and the very picture of respectability," Lady Bracknell retorts, "It is obviously the same person."

The Victorians wanted their art to contain a message, to provide guidance and support for right living. Hence Wilde makes Miss Prism, the governess, the embodiment of their conventional notions; she is a writer of three-decker novels in which "the good ended happily, and the bad unhappily. That is what Fiction means." Just as Wilde flicks his satiric whip at didactic art, so does he invert the "innocence" that Victorians demanded in their young ladies. He makes Cecily prefer distinctive manners to sound morals when she says to Algernon, "Yes, you've wonderfully good taste, Ernest. It's the excuse I've always given for your leading such a bad life."

To attempt to enumerate all or most of the instances in which the bubbling, effervescent dialogue touches with absurdity serious Victorian conventions would be to quote most of the play. To carry the analysis further would be to break the butterfly on the iron wheel, to dust the powder from the moth's wing with a clothes brush. Wilde's great contemporary Shaw fundamentally disapproved of what he considered to be Wilde's amoral nature, his too happy, irresponsible gaiety. Yet he greatly admired Wilde's supreme gifts as an entertainer. On hearing of Wilde's death, Shaw stated that he had gone straight to heaven, adding, "He is too good company to be excluded." It is his gift for light, bright amusement that constitutes the aesthetic center of the play, not the satire, which is merely the channel for the expression of the wit. Wilde perhaps best characterized the play when he referred to it modestly as a clever little thing "written by a butterfly for butterflies."

A POSTSCRIPT

Our discussion of the divergent satiric aims of plot and dialogue ought not to be closed without reference to the four-act version, somewhat longer than the present one which has been the basis of the acting tradition in English-speaking countries from the beginning. The New York Public Library in 1956 published its handsomely elegant Limited Edition of the longer version, "as Originally Written," along with an "Introduction" that gives the history of the texts. The longer text contains amusing scenes and dialogue not appearing in the now traditional version. There may be some difference of opinion as to which is the more entertaining version. Despite the interesting additional material, many will feel that the present version is superior in artistic neatness and verbal economy, that the action moves more smoothly and that the wit snaps and crackles a little more sharply—that it is a little less elaborately mannered in style.

There are, however, two scenes in the plot of the original text that add to the parody of conventional farce such as we have already adverted to. The two scenes are 1) an amusing scene turning on mistaken identity in which officers of the law arrive at the Manor House to arrest "Ernest Worthing" for a debt of several hundred pounds incurred at the luxurious Hotel Savoy in London. Although the indebtedness has been contracted by Jack

Worthing under the name of "Ernest," Algernon is at the moment in full stride in his impersonation of "brother Ernest." His success with Cecily will be undone if, in order to extricate himself from the threatening situation, he owns to being, not Ernest Worthing, but Algernon Moncrieff. The scene, of course, is handled with Wilde's usual bland indifference to implications and the everyday logic of human conduct. The second parody is a "take off" on another cliché of traditional comedy, the well-worn convention of the screen scene, such as we have in Goldsmith's *She Stoops to Conquer* and Sheridan's *The School for Scandal*. Algernon, supposedly paying a charity visit to the invalid Bunbury, is embarrassed by the sudden arrival at the Manor House of his aunt Lady Bracknell; he and Cecily retire behind a screen so that Wilde can burlesque this conventional stage situation.

As for the dialogue of the original text, it contains much more satire of the High Church movement towards restoring the precepts and practices of the Primitive Church. Most readers of today have forgotten how much the second half of the last century was troubled by "surplice riots" in churches and with court actions in restraint of those who were attempting to revive ancient rubrics and vestments, etc. Hence Dr. Chasuble (and with him, Miss Prism) has considerably more to say than in our version. At times the dialogue takes on a theological color as it turns on the spiritual merits of "baptismal regeneration" as opposed to more dramatic revivalist "conversions." Modern readers will have forgotten the sensational "Gorham case," a national scandal dealing with these ideas.

Some of the original humor becomes at moments sufficiently broad. For example, Dr. Chasuble enters to announce that the time has arrived for the christenings. Lady Bracknell, now present but unaware of all the fuss over the name of "Ernest," experiences a dignified but searching misgiving; she solemnly interrogates the assembled company as to the proper time-sequence in such matters, the propriety of christening babies before the marriage ceremonies have been performed. Obviously too much of this sort of humor can be overburdensome to the delicate fabric of the play as we have it; perhaps it is as well omitted.

To the biographer of Wilde, the four-act version may have a marginal interest. During the period of writing it, Wilde was in somewhat trying relations with Douglas, his nemesis. There is perhaps for this reason more than a humorously ironic overtone to thoughts and words referring to "profligacy," excessive eating and drinking, arrests and jails, to a type of "indolent and luxurious . . . first-class misdemeanant."

In 1957 Methuen and Co. of London published *The Original Four-Act Version of The Importance of Being Earnest with an Explanatory Foreword by Vyvyan Holland*. The Methuen-Holland version differs in some details from the New York Public Library four-act version. Although Holland suggests that his version is "the original" four-act play, critics would do well to read the more comprehensive and detailed Introduction to the New York Public Library version before accepting any final judgment on what is "the original" four-act text of *The Importance of Being Earnest*.

THE STAGING

The first seventy years of the nineteenth century were marked by very few memorable English plays. In trying to cater to popular taste, the theatrical producers allowed a progressive deterioration of standards until educated people seldom found much to enjoy in the theatre. Mid-century critics complained that not only did audiences demand the cheapest kind of amusement, but even that there was scarcely an actor in London who could play the part of a gentleman convincingly. From this we may gather that much had to be done before the English theatre was ready for the likes of Oscar Wilde.

The plays of the period consisted mainly of topical satires or spectacular melodramas in which battles, waterfalls, fires, and other sights played an important part. Although such productions may seem foolish when considered against the great tradition of English drama, they did introduce the concept of theatrical realism to English audiences for the first time. After all, the effectiveness of a spectacle is measured by the degree of illusion it attains. At first the new realism was of the crudest sort, but later it was refined and polished as audiences became more sophisticated. Eventually it was to produce that brilliant group of drawing-room comedies dating from the late Victorian period, of which *The Importance of Being Earnest* is such a distinguished example.

This new realism required the complete overthrow of all the old dramatic traditions. The plays of Shakespeare, Congreve, and Sheridan had been intended for a relatively stylized and unrealistic kind of presentation. Even during the eighteenth century when full stage settings were used for the first time, the scenery itself was mere background rather than an enclosure for the actor. Most of the action took place on an apron platform that projected out into the orchestra pit, thus bringing the actor

53

into the midst of the audience. This achieved intimacy, but at the expense of illusion. Concern for realism or even historical correctness was seldom felt. Everyday dress, with a few exceptions, was always worn, and one was apt to see the same columns, drawing room or park scene in play after play. These scenes were actually canvas panels on wooden frames and were called *wings*. Scene changes were effected by sliding them on and off stage in grooves. Detail, even including furniture, was simply painted on these wings.

The popular nineteenth century delight in sensational realism changed all this. As early as 1770 the great scene painter de Loutherbourg brought with him across the channel such realistic effects as fog, sunlight, moonlight, and even volcanic eruptions. Under his influence the proscenium arch became a gigantic picture frame which separated the audience from the magic but utterly real world beyond the footlights. It was but a short step from this sort of thing to the thrilling realism of spectacles like *The Cataract of the Ganges,* first produced in 1823 at Drury Lane, which was perhaps the most elaborate of the so-called "tank dramas" of the period.

But the emphasis on stage illusion was not entirely confined to spectacle and melodrama. A simultaneous development in plays with historical locales was the growing insistence on correct archaeological details. J. R. Planché was among the earliest technical advisers on this subject. In 1823 his researches resulted in a production of Shakespeare's *King John* at Covent Garden which, according to the playbill, was given "with an attention to costume never before equalled on the English stage. Every character will appear in the precise habit of the period; the whole of the decoration and dresses being executed from indisputable authorities, such as, monumental effigies, seals, illuminated manuscripts, etc."[1] While not every subsequent theatrical production was

---

[1] The bill for December 8, 1823, as reported in the *Theatrical Observer.* Quoted by Ernest Bradlee Watson, *Sheridan to Robertson,* Cambridge (Mass.): Harvard University Press, 1926, p. 263.

Plans showing transition from eighteenth-century wing-set to Madame Vestris' box set

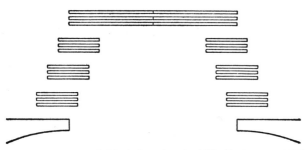

Wings placed one behind the other in 18th Century manner

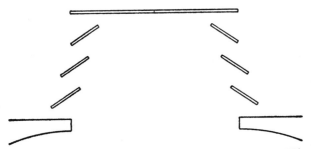

Wings "raked" or set at an angle (de Loutherbourg, c. 1770)

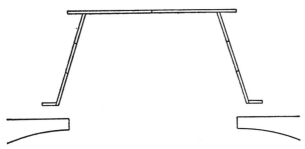

Wings turned all the way to the side, creating a box set

attended by such laudable historicism, the standards of stage illusion and plausibility continued to rise.

Another reformer, whose sphere was comedy, was Madame Eliza Vestris. She deserves a high place in the annals of the Victorian stage: beginning as an opera singer, she was soon even more famous as a comedienne. Later she became a theatre manager (we would say director and producer), a career which culminated in her taking over the great Covent Garden Theatre for a time. But it was at the little Olympic Theatre that Madame Vestris and her actor-husband, Charles Mathews, Jr., made their greatest strides in scenic reform. The eighteenth-century side wings had been "raked" or set at slight angles by de Loutherbourg so that they masked the backstage area more completely. (See diagram.) The next step, which was taken by Madame Vestris, was to increase this angle so that the side wings became actual walls and, together with the wings running across the back of the stage, formed three sides of a rectangular room. This was the first appearance of the familiar modern "box set."

With the advent of the box set, it became possible to increase the number of practicable doors and windows, and to apply three-dimensional moldings and draperies to the canvas walls, so that much less of the detail was painted. Madame Vestris also filled her stage with real and plausible furniture. Before her time such things had been unthinkable. The most bedraggled stool had served as a nobleman's armchair, and no furniture had appeared that was not actually used by the actors. Thus a state room in a royal palace might have been furnished only with one wobbly table and a couple of broken-down side chairs. There had been in no sense the "dressing" with unused but visually important props which is so important to plays like *The Importance of Being Earnest*.

Needless to say, this greater realism was achieved at the expense of scenic mobility. No longer could the painted flats slide on and off stage in their grooves, and no longer was the audience swiftly transported from the park to the drawing room and back several times within a single act. Madame Vestris' scenic reforms, as they were adopted by other managers, thus had an effect on play writing. Authors were forced to call for fewer and fewer scene changes. Wilde, for instance, gives us only one scene in each act, leaving the ample space of an intermission for each change of scene.

Madame Vestris and her husband also wrought significant changes in comic acting style. A greater naturalism in dress and manner brought to an end the long career of stylized clowns and comic types, many of them ultimately derived from the *Commedia dell' arte*. The conventionalized rakes and bumpkins of the seventeenth and eighteenth centuries were changed into lifelike and idiosyncratic people at the hands of these reformers.

Partly as a result of all these changes, play writing became once again a respectable art in England in the 1860's. The new conventions of historical accuracy, the realistic set decorated and lighted as if it were a real interior, and the breezy, natural manner of the new school of comedians set the stage (so to speak) for a revival of the drama and especially of high comedy. A brilliant period in the history of the English stage followed, graced by such figures as Shaw, Galsworthy, Archer, and Pinero.

One of the most brilliant of these late-Victorian dramatists was Oscar Wilde. How necessary for his plays was the realism of the new stage. As the curtain rises on the "morning-room" of Act One, the audience sees, not the stylized commonplaces of the typical "room in Lord ————'s house" which had been so familiar to the previous century, but a highly individualized and minutely studied late Victorian bachelor's flat. The room is influenced by the trend towards highly sensitive "good taste" which set in during the last years of Victoria's reign. The colors run to pale greens and browns, and perhaps there is a yellow border decorated with sunflowers above the picture rail. Underneath there is a panelled dado running around the room, perhaps four feet high and painted white. The walls are hung with large brown photographs of classical ruins and a few etchings or Aubrey Beardsley prints. The furniture is covered with rugs and batik cloths; everything is fringed, fronded, and foreign. There are Japanese whatnot cabinets, bamboo screens, tapa cloths from Polynesia, tall spiky iron lamps and lampshades studded with many-hued bits of glass. The windows are heavily mullioned and filled with stained glass. The fireplace is tiled and the mantel surmounted by a mirror which in turn is flanked by a display of Delft pottery.

The garden of Act Two reverts to the old-fashioned wing setting, with realistically painted oaks framing the stage, mortician's grass covering the floor (raised here and there by not-too-convincing hummocks in the lawn), a flower-bed of artificial flowers, and, at the back, a hedge to mask the bottom of the backdrop. Only the distant house painted on this backdrop is less than three-dimensional in effect. The noise of crickets filters out from the wings, and the new electric lighting system provides far more realistic sunbeams than de Loutherbourg ever dreamed possible. Tea is served on a frail but richly-wrought wicker table, and the ladies sit in enormous wicker chairs. There should be a croquet set in the middle distance.

The atmosphere of the drawing room in Act Three is that of a country house—a family place, and therefore not as modish as the room in Act One. Miss Prism's touch will be in evidence. The heavy lines of the 1870's will dominate the furniture which will be upholstered in plush or brocade. Antimacassars are to be seen, and gilt walnut and rosewood, rather than the stained oak which London would consider more "sincere" and which is certainly more *chic*. Rich draperies hang at the tall windows, which reach all the way to the floor so that you can walk through them into the garden, pushing aside the frothy lace curtains. The room is full of tiny tables covered with small, sentimental, and highly breakable objects: fragments of prehistoric bone, small china dogs, glass paperweights with little scenes inside them, Japanese paper fans, curious ebony carvings from Africa, doilies embroidered or crocheted, brass candle-snuffers, sewing-baskets, and limp-leather editions of Tennyson's *Maud*. The walls are covered with a fuzzy flock wallpaper in a strong pattern, and also with pictures, probably engravings of things like Landseer's *Dignity and Impudence* and Frith's *Derby Day*.

Whatever one might say of the taste of such rooms—and a good deal can be said in favor of it—there is no doubt that the theatre of realistic illusion has triumphed when we see them on the stage in such perfection. One might well be in a real garden, or country drawing-room, or city flat. No doubt the actors ate real muffins and drank real tea. The revolution that began with the "tank dramas," Madame Vestris, and J. R. Planché was completed in time for the plays of Oscar Wilde.

CAST OF CHARACTERS

JOHN WORTHING, J. P., of the Manor House, Woolton, Hertfordshire.
ALGERNON MONCRIEFF, his friend.

JACK

ALGERNON

CECILY

CHASUBLE

LADY BRACKNELL

GWENDOLEN

THE REVEREND CANON CHASUBLE, rector of Woolton.
LADY BRACKNELL, Algernon's aunt.
THE HONORABLE GWENDOLEN FAIRFAX, her daughter.
CECILY CARDEW, John Worthing's ward.
MISS PRISM, Cecily's governess.
MERRIMAN, a butler at John Worthing's Manor House.
LANE, a manservant, Algernon's "gentleman's gentleman."

SYNOPSIS OF SCENES

The action takes place in London and at a country house in Hertfordshire within the last decade of the nineteenth century.

ACT ONE

The morning-room in Algernon Moncrieff's flat in Half-Moon Street, London. [*Wilde's notes call for a door in the center of the left wall which would lead, presumably, to the outside door. Another door to the rear of the right hand wall opens to an adjoining room. Between it and the front of the stage is a highly ornamented fireplace.*] *The room is luxuriously and artistically furnished* [*in the mood of the aesthetic or "yellow decade"—Wilde reminiscences, such as blue and white china, Aubrey Beardsley drawings, some Japanese objets d'art, fragile chairs, etc. to give a rich, slightly ornate, cluttered effect.*] *The sound of a piano is heard in the adjoining room. Lane* [*Algernon's gentleman's gentleman*] *is arranging afternoon tea on the table, and after the music has ceased, Algernon enters* [*wearing meticulously correct stiff collar and cuffs, frock coat, delicately figured waistcoat, and striped trousers. All of the characters in the play conduct themselves with rigid decorum. Their unhurried gestures and movements are hallmarks of their rank and breeding. They speak with the polished and pointed elegance of a leisured society which valued brilliant, clever, amusing utterance.*][1]

---

[1] Unlike other dramatists presented in this series, Wilde is sufficiently modern to have inserted a considerable number of staging, acting, and reading guides. Additions to his text will appear in brackets. A more complete idea of this and later stage settings appears on pp. 57-59.

65

ALGERNON: [*wandering languidly in from the adjoining room and speaking in the sophisticated tone of mild ennui which is habitual to him*] Did you hear what I was playing, Lane?

LANE: [*his manner one of deferential respectfulness combined with dignified detachment; his is the quiet solemnity of a distantly tolling church-bell*] I didn't think it polite to listen, sir.

ALGERNON: I'm sorry for that, for your sake. I don't play accurately—anyone can play accurately—but I play with wonderful expression. As far as the piano is concerned, sentiment is my forte. I keep science for Life.

LANE: Yes, sir.

ALGERNON: And, speaking of the science of Life, have you got the cucumber sandwiches cut for Lady Bracknell?

LANE: Yes, sir. (*hands them on a salver*)

ALGERNON: (*inspects them, takes two, and sits down on the sofa*) Oh . . . by the WAY, Lane, I see from your book that on Thursday night when Lord Shoremen and Mr. Worthing were dining with me, eight bottles of champagne are entered as having been consumed.

LANE: Yes, sir; eight bottles and a pint.

ALGERNON: Why is it that at a bachelor's establishment the servants invariably drink the champagne? I ask merely for information.

LANE: I attribute it to the superior quality of the wine, sir. I have often observed that in married households the champagne is rarely of a first-rate brand.

ALGERNON: Good Heavens! Is marriage so demoralizing as that?

LANE: I believe it *is* a very pleasant state, sir. I have had very little experience of it myself up to the present. I have only been married once. That was in consequence of a misunderstanding between myself and a young woman.

ALGERNON: (*languidly*) I don't know that I am much interested in your family life, Lane.

LANE: No, sir; it is not a very interesting subject. I never think of it myself.

ALGERNON: Very natural, I am sure. That will do, Lane, thank you.

LANE: Thank you, sir.

Lane goes out [to left. Whether entering or leaving he moves with a stately gravity, a measured processional dignity.]

ALGERNON: Lane's views on marriage seem somewhat lax. Really, if the lower orders don't set us a good example, what on earth is the use of them? They seem, as a class, to have absolutely no sense of moral responsibility.

Lane enters [to announce a visitor.]

LANE: Mr. Ernest Worthing.

JACK: *[John Worthing] enters. He hands his top-hat and cane to Lane who accepts them with grave formality and goes out. [In conventional stage tradition, Jack is in general more conservative in dress and in manner than Algernon, cultivating more subdued waistcoats and a more restrained manner. Both agree in consuming leisure with a lavishness that assumes an almost Veblenesque dimension of "conspicuous consumption," and both have just the right touch of the insolent superiority of the true dandy. However, Jack as Cecily's guardian has assumed a dignity beyond his years. Indeed there is in his countenance the pallor and sobriety of a Church Warden or of a pessimistic minor poet trying to resemble a major one. He has a grave, masque-like sobriety of countenance, the faintest hint of muzziness and boredom about the corners of the eyes, the slightest touch of petulant weariness at the corners of the mouth, the most delicately suffused languor over the otherwise rigidly controlled features. This sets him off against Algy's more breezy and bouncy appearance, the latter having a sharp satiric look lying just beneath the surface of an engaging, playful look of innocent brightness, this expression being somewhat misleading and intended as such. Actually he is the less scrupulous of the two, informing us a few lines further that he does not intend to let his Bunbury perish after marriage regardless of how Jack disposes of Ernest.]*

ALGERNON: How are you, my dear Ernest? What brings you up to town?

JACK: [*speaking in the blasé tone of mild boredom habitual to him*] Oh, pleasure, pleasure! What else should bring one anywhere? Eating as usual, I see, Algy!

ALGERNON: (*stiffly*) I believe it is customary in good society to take some slight refreshment at five o'clock. Where have you been since last Thursday?

JACK: (*sitting down on the sofa*) In the country.

ALGERNON: What on earth do you do there?

JACK: (*pulling off his gloves*) When one is in town one amuses oneself. When one is in the country one amuses other people. It is excessively boring.

ALGERNON: And who are the people you amuse?

JACK: (*airily*) Oh, neighbors, neighbors.

ALGERNON: Got nice neighbors in your part of Shropshire?

JACK: Perfectly horrid! Never speak to one of them.

ALGERNON: How immensely you must amuse them! (*goes over and takes sandwich*) By the way, Shropshire is your county, is it not?

JACK: Eh? Shropshire? Yes, of course. Hallo! Why all these cups? Why cucumber sandwiches? Why such reckless extravagance in one so young? Who is coming to tea?

ALGERNON: Oh! merely Aunt Augusta and Gwendolen.

JACK: How perfectly delightful!

ALGERNON: Yes, that is all very well; but I am afraid Aunt Augusta won't quite approve of your being here.

JACK: May I ask why?

ALGERNON: My dear fellow, the way you flirt with Gwendolen is perfectly disgraceful. It is almost as bad as the way Gwendolen flirts with you.

JACK: [*staring with intense absorption at a sandwich, almost heedless of his words*] I am in love with Gwendolen. I have come up to town expressly to propose to her.

ALGERNON: I thought you had come up for pleasure? . . . I call that business.

JACK: How utterly unromantic you are!

ALGERNON: I really don't see anything romantic in

I am in love with Gwendolen.

proposing. It is very romantic to be in love. But there is nothing romantic about a definite proposal. Why, one may be accepted. One usually is, I believe. Then the excitement is all over. If ever I get married, I'll certainly try to forget the fact.

JACK: I have no doubt about that, dear Algy. The Divorce Court was specially invented for people whose memories are so curiously constituted.

ALGERNON: Oh! there is no use speculating on that subject. Divorces are made in Heaven—— (*Jack puts out his hand to take a sandwich. Algernon at once interferes.*) Please don't touch the cucumber sandwiches. They are ordered specially for Aunt Augusta. (*takes one and eats it*)

JACK: Well, you have been eating them all the time.

ALGERNON: That is quite a different matter. She is *my* aunt. (*takes plate from below*) Have some bread and butter. The bread and butter is for Gwendolen. Gwendolen is devoted to bread and butter.

JACK: (*advancing to table and helping himself*) And very good bread and butter it is, too.

ALGERNON: Well, my dear fellow, you need not eat as if you were going to eat it all. You are not married to her already, and I don't think you ever will be.

JACK: Why on earth do you say that?

ALGERNON: Well, in the first place girls never marry the men they flirt with. Girls don't think it right.

JACK: Oh, that is nonsense!

ALGERNON: It isn't. It is a great truth. It accounts for the extraordinary number of bachelors that one sees all over the place. In the second place, I don't give my consent.

JACK: Your consent!

ALGERNON: My dear fellow, Gwendolen is my first cousin. And before I allow you to marry her, you will have to clear up the whole question of Cecily. (*rings bell*)

JACK: Cecily! What on earth do you mean? What do you mean, Algy, by Cecily? I don't know anyone of the name of Cecily.

Lane enters.

ALGERNON: Bring me that cigarette case Mr. Worthing left in the smoking-room the last time he dined here.

LANE: Yes, sir. (*He goes out.*)

JACK: Do you mean to say you have had my cigarette case all this time? I wish to goodness you had let me know. I have been writing frantic letters to Scotland Yard[2] about it. I was very nearly offering a large reward.

ALGERNON: Well, I wish you would offer one. I happen to be more than usually hard up.

JACK: There is no good offering a large reward now that the thing is found.

Lane enters with the cigarette case on a salver. Algernon takes it at once. Lane goes out.

ALGERNON: I think that is rather mean of you, Ernest, I must say. (*opens case and examines it*) However, it makes no matter, for, now that I look at the inscription, I find that the thing isn't yours after all.

JACK: Of course it's mine. (*moving to him*) You have seen me with it a hundred times, and you have no right whatsoever to read what is written inside. It is a very ungentlemanly thing to read a private cigarette case.

ALGERNON: Oh! it is absurd to have a hard-and-fast rule about what one should read and what one shouldn't. More than half of modern culture depends on what one shouldn't read.

JACK: I am quite aware of the fact, and I don't propose to discuss modern culture. It isn't the sort of thing one should talk of in private. I simply want my cigarette case back.

ALGERNON: Yes; but this isn't your cigarette case. This cigarette case is a present from some one of the name of Cecily, and you said you didn't know any one of that name.

JACK: Well, if you want to know, Cecily happens to be my aunt.

ALGERNON: Your aunt!

---

[2] Headquarters of the metropolitan police.

JACK: Yes, charming old lady she is, too. Lives at Tunbridge Wells.[3] Just give it back to me, Algy.

ALGERNON: (*retreating to back of sofa*) But why does she call herself little Cecily if she is your aunt and lives at Tunbridge Wells? (*reading*) "From little Cecily with her fondest love."

JACK: (*moving to sofa and kneeling upon it*) My dear fellow, what on earth is there in that? Some aunts are tall, some aunts are not tall. That is a matter that surely an aunt may be allowed to decide for herself. You seem to think that every aunt should be exactly like your aunt! That is absurd! For Heaven's sake give me back my cigarette case. (*follows Algernon round the room*)

ALGERNON: Yes. But why does your aunt call you her uncle? "From little Cecily, with her fondest love to her dear Uncle Jack." There is no objection, I admit, to an aunt being a small aunt, but why an aunt, no matter what her size may be, should call her own nephew her uncle, I can't quite make out. Besides, your name isn't Jack at all; it is Ernest.

JACK: It isn't Ernest; it's Jack.

ALGERNON: You have always told me it was Ernest. I have introduced you to every one as Ernest. You answer to the name of Ernest. You look as if your name was Ernest. You are the most earnest looking person I ever saw in my life. It is perfectly absurd your saying that your name isn't Ernest. It's on your cards. Here is one of them. (*taking it from the case*) "Mr. Ernest Worthing, B 4, The Albany."[4] I'll keep this as a proof your name is Ernest

---

[3] A spa town in Kent, favored by retired elderly people.

[4] The subject of a novel *The Bachelor of the Albany* (1848), at which time it was a privileged sanctuary for bachelors and married men trying to live like bachelors. It religiously excluded "intrusive wives, disagreeable fathers, and importunate tradesmen." (—from the novel) An arcade of flats or chambers in West End London extending between Piccadilly and Burlington Gardens, it assumed the character, since 1812, of a peaceful backwater residence for the nobility and the gentry, a fashionable cloister for sedate and scholarly gentlemen and for discreet young men given to occasional and clandestine dissipation. Built origi-

if ever you attempt to deny it to me, or to Gwendolen, or to any one else. (*puts the card in his pocket*)

JACK: [*with impatient severity*] Well, my name is Ernest in town and Jack in the country, and the cigarette case was given to me in the country.

ALGERNON: Yes, but that does not account for the fact that your small Aunt Cecily, who lives at Tunbridge Wells, calls you her dear uncle. Come, old boy, you had much better have the thing out at once.

JACK: My dear Algy, you talk exactly as if you were a dentist. It is very vulgar to talk like a dentist when one isn't a dentist. It produces a false impression.

ALGERNON: Well, that is exactly what dentists always do. Now, go on! Tell me the whole thing. I may mention that I have always suspected you of being a confirmed and secret Bunburyist; and I am quite sure of it now.

JACK: Bunburyist? What on earth do you mean by a Bunburyist?

ALGERNON: I'll reveal to you the meaning of that incomparable expression as soon as you are kind enough to inform me why you are Ernest in town and Jack in the country.

JACK: Well, produce my cigarette case first.

ALGERNON: Here it is. (*hands [him] the cigarette case*) Now, produce your explanation, and pray make it improbable. (*He sits on sofa.*)

JACK: My dear fellow, there is nothing improbable about my explanation at all. In fact, it's perfectly ordinary. Old Mr. Thomas Cardew, who adopted me when I was a little boy, made me in his will guardian to his grand-daughter, Miss Cecily Cardew. Cecily, who addresses me as her uncle from motives of respect that you could not possibly appreciate, lives at my place in the

nally in 1774 as the town house of Lord Melbourne, it passed to the Duke of York and Albany (hence the name) and then was turned into residential chambers. Among its nineteenth-century inhabitants were Monk Lewis, Lord Byron, Bulwer Lytton, Thackeray, Gladstone (in his younger days), and Macaulay who lived there for fifteen years—where, surrounded by his 7,000 books, he wrote his famous *History*.

country under the charge of her admirable governess, Miss Prism.

ALGERNON: Where is that place in the country, by the way?

JACK: That is nothing to you, dear boy. You are not going to be invited. . . . I may tell you candidly that the place is not in Shropshire.

ALGERNON: I suspected that, my dear fellow! I have Bunburyed all over Shropshire on two separate occasions. Now, go on. Why are you Ernest in town and Jack in the country?

JACK: My dear Algy, I don't know whether you will be able to understand my real motives. You are hardly serious enough. When one is placed in the position of guardian, one has to adopt a very high moral tone on all subjects. It's one's duty to do so. And as a high moral tone can hardly be said to conduce very much to either one's health or one's happiness, in order to get up to town I have always pretended to have a younger brother of the name of Ernest, who lives in the Albany, and gets into the most dreadful scrapes. That, my dear Algy, is the whole truth pure and simple.

ALGERNON: The truth is rarely pure and never simple. Modern life would be very tedious if it were either, and modern literature a complete impossibility!

JACK: That wouldn't be at all a bad thing.

ALGERNON: Literary criticism is not your forte, my dear fellow. Don't try it. You should leave that to people who haven't been at a University. They do it so well in the daily papers. What you really are is a Bunburyist. I was quite right in saying you were a Bunburyist. You are one of the most advanced Bunburyists I know.

JACK: What on earth do you mean?

ALGERNON: You have invented a very useful younger brother called Ernest, in order that you may be able to come up to town as often as you like. I have invented an invaluable permanent invalid called Bunbury, in order that I may be able to go down into the country whenever I choose. Bunbury is perfectly invaluable. If it wasn't for

Bunbury's extraordinary bad health, for instance, I wouldn't be able to dine with you at Willis's[5] tonight, for I have been really engaged to Aunt Augusta for more than a week.

JACK: I haven't asked you to dine with me anywhere tonight.

ALGERNON: I know. You are absolutely careless about sending out invitations. It is very foolish of you. Nothing annoys people so much as not receiving invitations.

JACK: You had much better dine with your Aunt Augusta.

ALGERNON: I haven't the smallest intention of doing anything of the kind. To begin with, I dined there on Monday, and once a week is quite enough to dine with one's own relatives. In the second place, whenever I do dine there I am always treated as a member of the family, and sent down[6] with either no woman at all, or two. In the third place, I know perfectly well whom she will place me next to, tonight. She will place me next Mary Farquhar, who always flirts with her own husband across the dinner-table. That is not very pleasant. Indeed, it is not even decent . . . and that sort of thing is enormously on the increase. The amount of women in London who flirt with their own husbands is perfectly scandalous. It looks so bad. It is simply washing one's clean linen in public. Besides, now that I know you to be a confirmed Bunburyist I naturally want to talk to you about Bunburying. I want to tell you the rules.

JACK: I'm not a Bunburyist at all. If Gwendolen accepts me, I am going to kill my brother; indeed I think I'll kill him in any case. Cecily is a little too much interested in him. It is rather a bore. So I am going to get rid of Ernest. And I strongly advise you to do the same with

---

[5] A house noted as a place for entertainments and meetings, formerly known as Almack's, once a center of fashion, and located near the St. James Theatre where the *Importance* had its first performance.

[6] Invited to the dining table.

Mr. ———— with your invalid friend who has the absurd name.

ALGERNON: Nothing will induce me to part with Bunbury, and if you ever get married, which seems to me extremely problematic, you will be very glad to know Bunbury. A man who marries without knowing Bunbury has a very tedious time of it.

JACK: That is nonsense. If I marry a charming girl like Gwendolen, and she is the only girl I ever saw in my life that I would marry, I certainly won't want to know Bunbury.

ALGERNON: Then your wife will. You don't seem to realize, that in married life three is company and two is none.

JACK: (*sententiously*) That, my dear young friend, is the theory that the corrupt French Drama has been propounding for the last fifty years.

ALGERNON: Yes; and that the happy English home has proved in half the time.

JACK: For heaven's sake, don't try to be cynical. It's perfectly easy to be cynical.

ALGERNON: My dear fellow, it isn't easy to be anything now-a-days. There's such a lot of beastly competition about. (*The sound of an electric bell is heard.*) Ah! [*with a quiet shudder of exquisite sensibility*] that must be Aunt Augusta. Only relatives, or creditors, ever ring in that Wagnerian manner. Now, if I get her out of the way for ten minutes, so that you can have an opportunity for proposing to Gwendolen, may I dine with you tonight at Willis's?

JACK: I suppose so, if you want to.

ALGERNON: Yes, but you must be serious about it. I hate people who are not serious about meals. It is so shallow of them.

Lane enters.

LANE: [*announcing*] Lady Bracknell and Miss Fairfax.

Lady Bracknell and Gwendolen enter. [Lady Bracknell carries herself with the regal dignity bred in her by her ancestry, indoctrinated by childhood training, and bur-

nished by years of unquestioned domestic tyranny. *She has no trace of class superiority in its ordinary, conventional sense: she is no mere English matron ambitious of "status" because too unimaginative to pretend to anything else. There is, there can be, no question of her divine right to govern, to make all social arrangements. Her will is that of the cosmos, her tone that of an oracle, her manner as imperious as would be expected of one bearing the name of Augusta. Her attitude of total ascendency is rooted in the primitive innocence of her assumption of an inherent managerial prerogative. Her capacity for annihilating emphasis, calmly—without fuss or effort —is suggested by the fact that Lord Bracknell has been attenuated to an echo, a vapor. He does not appear because the husband of such a woman has only a nominal existence. She wears a large-brimmed hat with magnificent feather. Her beautiful black silk dress, black gloves, veil, parasol, chatelaine, and shoes are all in the most exquisite taste. Her daughter Gwendolen displays in periodfashion luxuriant mounds of hair; her blouse is highnecked; her jacket has sleeves ballooning at the shoulders in the approved leg-of-mutton style; skirts are long and voluminous. The waist is of the "hour-glass" or "wasp" type, achieved not without a little tight lacing. Her parasol, frilly and fashionable, has a long, elegant handle. She is the essence of that urban creation, the stylishly bored young lady. Her voice is tuned to a languorous, drawingroom drawl, a contralto just a trifly husky, imparting a touch of humor to her utterance. A young lady of obviously fastidious breeding and tailoring, she is her mother's daughter, self-confident and self-possessed.*] *Algernon goes forward to meet them.*

LADY BRACKNELL: [*in the firm and rather deep voice to which her age and position entitle her*] Good afternoon, dear Algernon, I hope you are behaving very well.

ALGERNON: I'm feeling very well, Aunt Augusta.

LADY BRACKNELL: That's not quite the same thing. In fact the two things rarely go together. (*sees Jack and bows to him with icy coldness*)

ALGERNON: (*to Gwendolen*) Dear me, you are smart!

GWENDOLEN: [*in her habitual tone of aristocratic and worldly superiority accompanied by a faint trace of boredom*] I am always smart! Aren't I, Mr. Worthing?

JACK: You're quite perfect, Miss Fairfax.

GWENDOLEN: Oh! I hope I am not that. It would leave no room for developments, and I intend to develop in many directions. (*Gwendolen and Jack sit down together in the corner.*)

LADY BRACKNELL: I'm sorry if we are a little late, Algernon, but I was obliged to call on dear Lady Harbury. I hadn't been there since her poor husband's death. I never saw a woman so altered; she looks quite twenty years younger. And now I'll have a cup of tea, and one of those nice cucumber sandwiches you promised me.

ALGERNON: Certainly, Aunt Augusta. (*goes over to tea-table*)

LADY BRACKNELL: [*arranging herself on the sofa*] Won't you come and sit here, Gwendolen?

GWENDOLEN: Thanks, mamma, I'm quite comfortable where I am.

ALGERNON: (*picking up an empty plate in horror*) Good heavens! Lane! Why are there no cucumber sandwiches? I ordered them specially.

LANE: (*gravely*) There were no cucumbers in the market this morning, sir. I went down twice.

ALGERNON: No cucumbers!

LANE: No, sir. Not even for ready money.

ALGERNON: That will do, Lane, thank you.

LANE: Thank you, sir. (*He goes out.*)

ALGERNON: I am greatly distressed, Aunt Augusta, about there being no cucumbers, not even for ready money.

LADY BRACKNELL: It really makes no matter, Algernon. I had some crumpets with Lady Harbury, who seems to me to be living entirely for pleasure now.

ALGERNON: I hear her hair has turned quite gold from grief.

LADY BRACKNELL: It certainly has changed its color.

From what cause I, of course, cannot say. (*Algernon crosses and hands tea.*) Thank you. I've quite a treat for you tonight, Algernon. I am going to send you down with Mary Farquhar. She is such a nice woman, and so attentive to her husband. It's delightful to watch them.

ALGERNON: I am afraid, Aunt Augusta, I shall have to give up the pleasure of dining with you tonight after all.

LADY BRACKNELL: (*frowning*) I hope not, Algernon. It would put my table completely out. Your uncle would have to dine upstairs. Fortunately he is accustomed to that.

ALGERNON: It is a great bore, and, I need hardly say, a terrible disappointment to me, but the fact is I have just had a telegram to say that my poor friend Bunbury is very ill again. (*exchanges glances with Jack*) They seem to think I should be with him.

LADY BRACKNELL: It is very strange. This Mr. Bunbury seems to suffer from curiously bad health.

ALGERNON: Yes; poor Bunbury is a dreadful invalid.

LADY BRACKNELL: Well, I must say, Algernon, that I think it is high time that Mr. Bunbury made up his mind whether he was going to live or to die. [*in a tone of indignant impatience*] This shilly-shallying with the question is absurd. Nor do I in any way approve of the modern sympathy with invalids. I consider it morbid. Illness of any kind is hardly a thing to be encouraged in others. Health is the primary duty of life. I am always telling that to your poor uncle, but he never seems to take much notice . . . as far as any improvement in his ailments goes. I should be much obliged if you would ask Mr. Bunbury, from me, to be kind enough not to have a relapse on Saturday, for I rely on you to arrange my music for me. It is my last reception and one wants something that will encourage conversation, particularly at the end of the season when everyone has practically said whatever they had to say, which, in most cases, was probably not much.

ALGERNON: I'll speak to Bunbury, Aunt Augusta, if he is still conscious, and I think I can promise you he'll be all right by Saturday. You see, if one plays good music, people don't listen, and if one plays bad music people don't talk. But I'll run over the program I've drawn out, if you will kindly come into the next room for a moment. [*He starts off to the right.*]

LADY BRACKNELL: Thank you, Algernon. It is very thoughtful of you. (*rising, and following Algernon*) I'm sure the program will be delightful, after a few expurgations. French songs I cannot possibly allow. People always seem to think that they are improper, and either look shocked, which is vulgar, or laugh, which is worse. But German sounds a thoroughly respectable language, and indeed, I believe is so. Gwendolen, you will accompany me.

GWENDOLEN: Certainly, mamma. (*Lady Bracknell and Algernon go into the music-room; Gwendolen remains behind.*)

JACK: Charming day it has been, Miss Fairfax.

GWENDOLEN: Pray don't talk to me about the weather, Mr. Worthing. Whenever people talk to me about the weather, I always feel quite certain that they mean something else. And that makes me so nervous.

JACK: I do mean something else.

GWENDOLEN: I thought so. In fact, I am never wrong.

JACK: And I would like to be allowed to take advantage of Lady Bracknell's temporary absence . . .

GWENDOLEN: I would certainly advise you to do so. Mamma has a way of coming back suddenly into a room that I have often had to speak to her about.

JACK: (*nervously*) [—*but with an exaggerated impulsiveness not entirely genuine*] Miss Fairfax, ever since I met you I have admired you more than any girl . . . I have ever met since . . . I met you.

GWENDOLEN: [*with the official self-composure of one making an important public announcement*] Yes, I am quite aware of the fact. And I often wish that in public, at any rate, you had been more demonstrative. For me you have always had an irresistible fascination. Even before I met you I was far from indifferent to you. (*Jack looks at her in amazement.*) We live, as I hope you know,

Mr. Worthing, in an age of ideals. The fact is constantly mentioned in the more expensive monthly magazines, and has reached the provincial pulpits I am told: and my ideal has always been to love some one of the name of Ernest. There is something in that name that inspires absolute confidence. The moment Algernon first mentioned to me that he had a friend called Ernest, I knew I was destined to love you.

JACK: You really love me, Gwendolen?

GWENDOLEN: [*with cool, distant absent-mindedness*] Passionately!

JACK: [*factual and calm*] Darling! You don't know how happy you've made me.

GWENDOLEN: My own dear Ernest!

JACK: But you don't really mean to say that you couldn't love me if my name wasn't Ernest?

GWENDOLEN: But your name is Ernest.

JACK: Yes, I know it is. But supposing it was something else? Do you mean to say you couldn't love me then?

GWENDOLEN: (*glibly*) Ah! that is clearly a metaphysical speculation, and like most metaphysical speculations has very little reference at all to the actual facts of real life, as we know them.

JACK: Personally, darling, to speak quite candidly, I don't much care about the name of Ernest . . . I don't think that name suits me at all.

GWENDOLEN: It suits you perfectly. It is a divine name. It has a music of its own. It produces vibrations.

JACK: Well, really, Gwendolen, I must say that I think there are lots of other much nicer names. I think, Jack, for instance, a charming name.

GWENDOLEN: Jack? . . . No, there is very little music in the name Jack, if any at all, indeed. It does not thrill. It produces absolutely no vibrations. . . . I have known several Jacks, and they all, without exception, were more than usually plain. Besides, Jack is a notorious domesticity for John! And I pity any woman who is married to a man called John. She would probably never be allowed to know the entrancing pleasure of a single moment's solitude. The only really safe name is Ernest.

JACK: Gwendolen, I must get christened at once—I mean we must get married at once. There is no time to be lost.

GWENDOLEN: Married, Mr. Worthing?

JACK: (*astounded*) Well . . . surely. You know that I love you, and you led me to believe, Miss Fairfax, that you were not absolutely indifferent to me.

GWENDOLEN: I adore you. But you haven't proposed to me yet. Nothing has been said at all about marriage. The subject has not even been touched on.

JACK: Well . . . may I propose to you now?

GWENDOLEN: I think it would be an admirable opportunity. And to spare you any possible disappointment, Mr. Worthing, I think it only fair to tell you quite frankly beforehand that I am fully determined to accept you.

JACK: Gwendolen!

GWENDOLEN: Yes, Mr. Worthing, what have you got to say to me?

JACK: You know what I have got to say to you.

GWENDOLEN: Yes, but you don't say it.

JACK: Gwendolen, will you marry me? (*goes on his knees*)

GWENDOLEN: Of course I will darling. How long you have been about it! I am afraid you have had very little experience in how to propose.

JACK: My own one, I have never loved any one in the world but you.

GWENDOLEN: Yes, but men often propose for practice. I know my brother Gerald does. All my girl-friends tell me so. What wonderfully blue eyes you have, Ernest! They are quite, quite blue. I hope you will always look at me just like that, especially when there are other people present.

Lady Bracknell enters.

LADY BRACKNELL: [*thundering out of Zion*] Mr. Worthing! Rise, sir, from this semi-recumbent posture. It is most indecorous.

I feel bound to tell you that you are not down on my list of eligible young men . . .

GWENDOLEN: Mamma! (*He tries to rise; she restrains him.*) I must beg you to retire. This is no place for you. Besides, Mr. Worthing has not quite finished yet.

LADY BRACKNELL: Finished what, may I ask?

GWENDOLEN: I am engaged to Mr. Worthing, mamma. (*They rise together.*)

LADY BRACKNELL: Pardon me, you are not engaged to any one. When you do become engaged to some one, I, or your father, should his health permit him, will inform you of the fact. An engagement should come on a young girl as a surprise, pleasant or unpleasant, as the case may be. It is hardly a matter that she could be allowed to arrange for herself. . . . And now I have a few questions to put to you, Mr. Worthing. While I am making these inquiries, you, Gwendolen, will wait for me below in the carriage.

GWENDOLEN: (*reproachfully*) Mamma!

LADY BRACKNELL: In the carriage, Gwendolen! (*Gwendolen goes to the door. She and Jack blow kisses to each other behind Lady Bracknell's back. Lady Bracknell looks vaguely about as if she could not understand what the noise was. She finally turns round.*) Gwendolen, the carriage!

GWENDOLEN: Yes, mamma. (*She goes out, looking back at Jack.*)

LADY BRACKNELL: (*sitting down*) You can take a seat, Mr. Worthing. (*looks in her pocket for a note-book and pencil*)

JACK: Thank you, Lady Bracknell, I prefer standing.

LADY BRACKNELL: (*pencil and note-book in hand*) [*with the high yet business-like severity of a bishop examining a candidate for orders*] I feel bound to tell you that you are not down on my list of eligible young men, although I have the same list as the dear Duchess of Bolton has. We work together, in fact. However, I am quite ready to enter your name, should your answers be what a really affectionate mother requires. Do you smoke?

JACK: Well, yes, I must admit I smoke.

LADY BRACKNELL: [*with a touch of enthusiasm rare with her*] I am glad to hear it. A man should always have an occupation of some kind. There are far too many idle men in London as it is. How old are you?

JACK: Twenty-nine.

LADY BRACKNELL: A very good age to be married at. I have always been of opinion that a man who desires to get married should know either everything or nothing. Which do you know?

JACK: (*after some hesitation*) I know nothing, Lady Bracknell.

LADY BRACKNELL: I am pleased to hear it. I do not approve of anything that tampers with natural ignorance. Ignorance is like a delicate exotic fruit; touch it and the bloom is gone. The whole theory of modern education is radically unsound. Fortunately in England, at any rate, education produces no effect whatsoever. If it did, it would prove a serious danger to the upper classes, and probably lead to acts of violence in Grosvenor Square.[7] What is your income?

JACK: Between seven and eight thousand a year.

LADY BRACKNELL: (*makes a note in her book*) In land, or in investments?

JACK: In investments, chiefly.

LADY BRACKNELL: That is satisfactory. What between the duties expected of one during one's life-time, and the duties exacted from one after one's death, land has ceased to be either a profit or a pleasure. It gives one position, and prevents one from keeping it up. That's all that can be said about land.

JACK: I have a country house with some land, of course, attached to it, about fifteen hundred acres, I believe; but I don't depend on that for my real income. In fact, as far as I can make out, the poachers are the only people who make anything out of it.

LADY BRACKNELL: A country house! How many bedrooms? Well, that point can be cleared up afterwards

---

[7] A fashionable residential area.

You have a town house, I hope? A girl with a simple, unspoiled nature, like Gwendolen, could hardly be expected to reside in the country.

JACK: Well, I own a house in Belgrave Square,[7] but it is let by the year to Lady Bloxham. Of course, I can get it back whenever I like, at six months' notice.

LADY BRACKNELL: Lady Bloxham? I don't know her.

JACK: Oh, she goes about very little. She is a lady considerably advanced in years.

LADY BRACKNELL: Ah, now-a-days that is no guarantee of respectability of character. What number in Belgrave Square?

JACK: 149.

LADY BRACKNELL: (*shaking her head*) The unfashionable side. I thought there was something. However, that could easily be altered.

JACK: [*in a tone of artless, inquiring innocence*] Do you mean the fashion, or the side?

LADY BRACKNELL: (*sternly*) Both, if necessary, I presume. What are your politics?

JACK: Well, I am afraid I really have none. I am a Liberal Unionist.[8]

LADY BRACKNELL: Oh, they count as Tories. They dine with us. Or come in the evening, at any rate. Now to minor matters. Are your parents living?

JACK: I have lost both my parents.

LADY BRACKNELL: Both? . . . That seems like carelessness. Who was your father? He was evidently a man of some wealth. Was he born in what the Radical papers call the purple of commerce, or did he rise from the ranks of the aristocracy?

JACK: I am afraid I really don't know. The fact is, Lady Bracknell, I said I had lost my parents. It would be nearer the truth to say that my parents seem to have lost me . . . I don't actually know who I am by birth. I was . . . well, I was found.

---

[8] The faction of the Liberal Party that seceded in 1886 because, like the conservatives, they wished to keep all of Ireland within the British Empire.

LADY BRACKNELL: Found!

JACK: The late Mr. Thomas Cardew, an old gentleman of a very charitable and kindly disposition, found me, and gave me the name of Worthing, because he happened to have a first-class ticket for Worthing in his pocket at the time. Worthing is a place in Sussex. It is a seaside resort.

LADY BRACKNELL: Where did the charitable gentleman who had a first-class ticket for this seaside resort find you?

JACK: (*gravely*) In a hand-bag.

LADY BRACKNELL: A hand-bag?

JACK: (*very seriously*) Yes, Lady Bracknell. I was in a hand-bag—a somewhat large, black leather hand-bag, with handles to it—an ordinary hand-bag in fact.

LADY BRACKNELL: In what locality did this Mr. James, or Thomas, Cardew come across this ordinary hand-bag?

JACK: In the cloak-room at Victoria Station. It was given to him in mistake for his own.

LADY BRACKNELL: The cloak-room at Victoria Station?

JACK: [*with deliberately oppressive honesty*] Yes. The Brighton line.

LADY BRACKNELL: The line is immaterial. [*moved to perorative sonorousness*] Mr. Worthing, I confess I feel somewhat bewildered by what you have just told me. To be born, or at any rate bred, in a hand-bag, whether it had handles or not, seems to me to display a contempt for the ordinary decencies of family life that remind one of the worst excesses of the French Revolution. And I presume you know what that unfortunate movement led to? As for the particular locality in which the hand-bag was found, a cloak-room at a railway station might serve to conceal a social indiscretion—has probably, indeed, been used for that purpose before now—but it could hardly be regarded as an assured basis for a recognized position in good society.

JACK: May I ask you then what you would advise me to do? I need hardly say I would do anything in the world to ensure Gwendolen's happiness.

LADY BRACKNELL: [*modulating into withering forthrightness*] I would strongly advise you, Mr. Worthing, to try and acquire some relations as soon as possible, and to make definite effort to produce at any rate one parent, of either sex, before the season is quite over.

JACK: [*with a primitive unconcern for Lady Bracknell's social demands*] Well, I don't see how I could possibly manage to do that. I can produce the hand-bag at any moment. It is in my dressing-room at home. I really think that should satisfy you, Lady Bracknell.

LADY BRACKNELL: [*as though contemplating an obscene horror*] Me, sir! What has it to do with me? You can hardly imagine that I and Lord Bracknell would dream of allowing our only daughter—a girl brought up with the utmost care—to marry into a cloak-room, and form an alliance with a parcel? Good morning, Mr. Worthing! (*Lady Bracknell sweeps out in majestic indignation.*)

JACK: Good morning! (*Algernon, from the other room, strikes up the Wedding March. Jack looks perfectly furious, and goes to the door.*) For goodness' sake don't play that ghastly tune, Algy! How idiotic you are! (*The music stops, and Algernon enters cheerily.*)

ALGERNON: Didn't it go off all right, old boy? You don't mean to say Gwendolen refused you? I know it is a way she has. She is always refusing people. I think it is most ill-natured of her.

JACK: Oh, Gwendolen is as right as a trivet. As far as she is concerned, we are engaged. Her mother is perfectly unbearable. Never met such a Gorgon . . . I don't really know what a Gorgon[9] is like, but I am quite sure that Lady Bracknell is one. In any case, she is a monster, without being a myth, which is rather unfair. . . . I beg your pardon, Algy, I suppose I shouldn't talk about your own aunt in that way before you.

ALGERNON: My dear boy, I love hearing my relations abused. It is the only thing that makes me put up with

---

[9] If he really doesn't, he stumbled on a good comparison since a Gorgon was one of the three sisters of Greek mythology whose hair was composed of snakes and whose glance turned the beholder into stone.

them at all. Relations are simply a tedious pack of people, who haven't got the remotest knowledge of how to live, nor the smallest instinct about when to die.

JACK: Oh, that is nonsense!

ALGERNON: It isn't!

JACK: Well, I won't argue about the matter. You always want to argue about things.

ALGERNON: That is exactly what things were originally made for.

JACK: Upon my word, if I thought that, I'd shoot myself . . . (*a pause*) You don't think there is any chance of Gwendolen becoming like her mother in about a hundred and fifty years, do you, Algy?

ALGERNON: All women become like their mothers. That is their tragedy. No man does. That's his.

JACK: Is that clever?

ALGERNON: It is perfectly phrased! and quite as true as any observation in civilized life should be.

JACK: I am sick to death of cleverness. Everybody is clever now-a-days. You can't go anywhere without meeting clever people. The thing has become an absolute public nuisance. I wish to goodness we had a few fools left.

ALGERNON: We have.

JACK: I should extremely like to meet them. What do they talk about?

ALGERNON: The fools? Oh! about the clever people, of course.

JACK: What fools!

ALGERNON: By the way, did you tell Gwendolen the truth about your being Ernest in town, and Jack in the country?

JACK: (*in a very patronizing manner*) My dear fellow, the truth isn't quite the sort of thing one tells to a nice, sweet, refined girl. What extraordinary ideas you have about the way to behave to a woman!

ALGERNON: [*affecting a youthfully rakish glitter in the eyes*] The only way to behave to a woman is to make love to her, if she is pretty, and to some one else if she is plain.

JACK: Oh, that is nonsense.

ALGERNON: What about your brother? What about the profligate Ernest?

JACK: Oh, before the end of the week I shall have got rid of him. I'll say he died in Paris of apoplexy. Lots of people die of apoplexy, quite suddenly, don't they?

ALGERNON: Yes, but it's hereditary, my dear fellow. It's the sort of thing that runs in families. You had much better say a severe chill.

JACK: You are sure a severe chill isn't hereditary, or anything of that kind?

ALGERNON: Of course it isn't!

JACK: Very well, then. My poor brother Ernest is carried off suddenly in Paris, by a severe chill. That gets rid of him.

ALGERNON: But I thought you said that . . . Miss Cardew was a little too much interested in your poor brother Ernest? Won't she feel his loss a good deal?

JACK: Oh, that is all right. Cecily is not a silly, romantic girl, I am glad to say. She has got a capital appetite, goes for long walks, and pays no attention at all to her lessons.

ALGERNON: I would rather like to see Cecily.

JACK: I will take very good care you never do. She is excessively pretty, and she is only just eighteen.

ALGERNON: Have you told Gwendolen yet that you have an excessively pretty ward who is only just eighteen?

JACK: Oh, one doesn't blurt these things out to people. Cecily and Gwendolen are perfectly certain to be extremely great friends. I'll bet you anything you like that half an hour after they have met, they will be calling each other sister.

ALGERNON: Women only do that when they have called each other a lot of other things first. Now, my dear boy, if we want to get a good table at Willis's, we really must go and dress. Do you know it is nearly seven?

JACK: (*irritably*) Oh, it always is nearly seven.

ALGERNON: Well, I'm hungry.

JACK: I never knew you when you weren't. . . .

ALGERNON: What shall we do after dinner? Go to a theater?

JACK: Oh, no! I loathe listening.

ALGERNON: Well, let us go to the Club?

JACK: Oh, no! I hate talking.

ALGERNON: Well, we might trot round to the Empire[10] at ten?

JACK: Oh, no! I can't bear looking at things. It is so silly.

ALGERNON: Well, what shall we do?

JACK: Nothing!

ALGERNON: It is awfully hard work doing nothing. However, I don't mind hard work where there is no definite object of any kind.

Lane enters.

LANE: Miss Fairfax.

Gwendolen enters. Lane goes out.

ALGERNON: Gwendolen, upon my word!

GWENDOLEN: Algy, kindly turn your back. I have something very particular to say to Mr. Worthing.

ALGERNON: Really, Gwendolen, I don't think I can allow this at all.

GWENDOLEN: Algy, you always adopt a strictly immoral attitude towards life. You are not quite old enough to do that. (*Algernon retires to the fireplace.*)

JACK: My own darling!

GWENDOLEN: Ernest, we may never be married. From the expression on mamma's face I fear we never shall. Few parents now-a-days pay any regard to what their children say to them. The old-fashioned respect for the young is fast dying out. Whatever influence I ever had over mamma, I lost at the age of three. But although she may prevent us from becoming man and wife, and I may marry some one else, and marry often, nothing that she can possibly do can alter my eternal devotion to you.

---

[10] A relatively new London theatre noted for the production of "spectacles" like *Around the World in 80 Days*. Opening in Leicester Square in 1883, it became a variety theatre a little later.

JACK: [*with a look of mock admiration and romantic nostalgia*] Dear Gwendolen.

GWENDOLEN: [*with subdued operatic grandeur of style*] The story of your romantic origin, as related to me by mamma, with unpleasing comments, has naturally stirred the deeper fibers of my nature. Your Christian name has an irresistible fascination. The simplicity of your character makes you exquisitely incomprehensible to me. Your town address at the Albany I have. What is your address in the country?

JACK: The Manor House, Woolton, Hertfordshire. (*Algernon, who has been carefully listening, smiles to himself, and writes the address on his shirt-cuff. He then picks up the Railway Guide.*)

GWENDOLEN: There is good postal service, I suppose? It may be necessary to do something desperate. That, of course, will require serious consideration. I will communicate with you daily.

JACK: My own one!

GWENDOLEN: How long do you remain in town?

JACK: Till Monday.

GWENDOLEN: Good! Algy, you may turn round now.

ALGERNON: Thanks, I've turned round already.

GWENDOLEN: You may also ring the bell. [*Algernon obeys.*]

JACK: You will let me see you to your carriage, my own darling?

GWENDOLEN: Certainly.

JACK: (*to Lane, who now enters*) I will see Miss Fairfax out.

LANE: Yes, sir. (*Jack and Gwendolen go off. Lane presents several letters on a salver to Algernon. It is to be surmised that they are bills, as Algernon, after looking at the envelopes, tears them up.*)

ALGERNON: A glass of sherry, Lane.

LANE: Yes, sir.

ALGERNON: Tomorrow, Lane, I'm going Bunburying.

LANE: Yes, sir.

ALGERNON: I shall probably not be back till Monday.

You can put up my dress clothes, my smoking jacket, and all the Bunbury suits . . .

LANE: Yes, sir. (*handing the sherry*)

ALGERNON: I hope tomorrow will be a fine day, Lane.

LANE: It never is, sir.

ALGERNON: Lane, you're a perfect pessimist.

LANE: I do my best to give satisfaction, sir.

Jack enters. Lane goes off.

JACK: There's a sensible, intellectual girl! the only girl I ever cared for in my life. (*Algernon is laughing immoderately.*) What on earth are you so amused at?

ALGERNON: Oh, I'm a little anxious about poor Bunbury, that's all.

JACK: If you don't take care, your friend Bunbury will get you into a serious scrape some day.

ALGERNON: I love scrapes. They are the only things that are never serious.

JACK: Oh, that's nonsense, Algy. You never talk anything but nonsense.

ALGERNON: Nobody ever does.

Jack looks indignantly at him, and leaves the room [through the door to right]. Algernon lights a cigarette, reads his shirt-cuff and smiles.

CURTAIN

ACT TWO

The garden at the Manor House. A flight of gray stone steps leads up to the house. The garden, an old-fashioned one, is full of roses. The time of year is July. Basket chairs, and a table covered with books, are set under a large yew tree. Miss Prism is seated at the table. [She is the perfect British governess, exact and correct in manner as she is in costume. Her starched white shirtwaist is set off by a narrow black ribbon tied in a bow around her collar, the black cord of her black-rimmed pince-nez, black skirt, and black shoes—also black stockings if they could be seen. Her countenance is one of cultivated severity and strenuous ethical refinement. Her tone of voice and turn of phrase are always normative and didactic. Her passions have the dignity and disadvantage of being —in appearance—entirely and narrowly ethical. Actually she is a spinster-governess on the straight-and-narrow but with an eye open for a marital side-lane ending in a country rectory.] Cecily is at the back, watering flowers. [In her light-colored summer dress, she appears even younger than she is, an effect which is adumbrated by her demure and childishly straightforward manner. She radiates the youthful charm of impregnable innocence and naive certainty about what she knows to be true. Her simple, open-air freshness of style and manner do not entirely conceal a determined and confident nature. In mental resource she is easily a match for Algernon or Gwendolen. Which reminds us that we are in a House-and-Garden "country," that is, London disguised with trees and shrubs.]

MISS PRISM: (*calling*) Cecily, Cecily! Surely such a utilitarian occupation as the watering of flowers is rather Moulton's duty than yours? Especially at a moment when intellectual pleasures await you. Your German grammar is on the table. Pray open it at page fifteen. We will repeat yesterday's lesson.

CECILY: (*coming over very slowly*) But I don't like German. It isn't at all a becoming language. I know perfectly well that I look quite plain after my German lesson.

MISS PRISM: Child, you know how anxious your guardian is that you should improve yourself in every way. He laid particular stress on your German, as he was leaving for town yesterday. Indeed, he always lays stress on your German when he is leaving for town.

CECILY: Dear Uncle Jack is so very serious! Sometimes he is so serious that I think he cannot be quite well.

MISS PRISM: (*drawing herself up*) Your guardian enjoys the best of health, and his gravity of demeanor is especially to be commended in one so comparatively young as he is. I know no one who has a higher sense of duty and responsibility.

CECILY: I suppose that is why he often looks a little bored when we three are together.

MISS PRISM: Cecily! I am surprised at you. Mr. Worthing has many troubles in his life. Idle merriment and triviality would be out of place in his conversation. You must remember his constant anxiety about that unfortunate young man, his brother.

CECILY: I wish Uncle Jack would allow that unfortunate young man, his brother, to come down here sometimes. We might have a good influence over him, Miss Prism. I am sure you certainly would. You know German, and geology, and things of that kind influence a man very much. (*She begins to write in her diary.*)

MISS PRISM: (*shaking her head*) I do not think that even I could produce any effect on a character that, according to his own brother's admission, is irretrievably weak and vacillating. Indeed, I am not sure that I would desire to reclaim him. I am not in favor of this modern mania for turning bad people into good people at a moment's notice. As a man sows so let him reap. You must put away your diary, Cecily. I really don't see why you should keep a diary at all.

CECILY: I keep a diary in order to enter the wonderful secrets of my life. If I didn't write them down I should probably forget all about them.

MISS PRISM: Memory, my dear Cecily, is the diary that we all carry about with us.

CECILY: Yes, but it usually chronicles the things that have never happened, and couldn't possibly have happened. I believe that Memory is responsible for nearly all the three-volume novels that Mudie[1] sends us.

MISS PRISM: Do not speak slightingly of the three-volume novel, Cecily. I wrote one myself in earlier days.

CECILY: Did you really, Miss Prism? How wonderfully clever you are! I hope it did not end happily? I don't like novels that end happily. They depress me so much.

MISS PRISM: The good ended happily, and the bad unhappily. That is what Fiction means.

CECILY: I suppose so. But it seems very unfair. And was your novel ever published?

MISS PRISM: Alas! no. The manuscript unfortunately was abandoned. I use the word in the sense of lost or mislaid. To your work, child, these speculations are profitless.

CECILY: (*smiling*) But I see Dr. Chasuble coming up through the garden.

MISS PRISM: (*rising and advancing*) Dr. Chasuble! This is indeed a pleasure.

Canon Chasuble enters. [*Dressed becomingly in clerical garb and wearing a pince-nez as if in token of his scholarly and serious nature, he comports himself with the directness and authority of a man approaching middle age and secure in his calling. He speaks with only the faintest trace of unctuousness. As his name indicates, the Rev. Chasuble was educated—presumably at Oxford—*

---

[1] A well-known London lending library.

when the High-Church revival was in its ritualistic phase. No doubt, for a time after taking his degree, he was a Fellow at one of the less intellectual colleges where he tarried, waiting for an appointment to a pleasant country living. One feels that, without any pain of uprooting, he has gently drifted from the port and gossip of the Common Room to the port and partridge of the Rectory. Although a man quite devoid of subtle perceptions, he is not so wholly unworldly and unsophisticated as to belong to what has been called the "lovable innocent" type of parson presented, for example, in the Vicar of Wakefield. *In ecclesiastical temperament he is ritualistic because vestments and altar ornaments are less difficult to comprehend than abstruse theology; his fondness for the "primitive Church" is sentimental antiquarianism, not historical passion. He likes mysticism, not because of a devotional temper but simply because he is vague and indefinite. His fondness for celibacy is born neither of fastidiousness or asceticism; it is a creature of self-indulgence: a wife and family might be a bore, certainly a bother. He is nothing if not obliging and sympathetic. He is composed of bland equanimity qualified by a tranquil incuriousness. He would be the perfect chaplain for a Society for the Enjoyment of Rural Leisure.*]

CANON CHASUBLE: And how are we this morning? Miss Prism, you are, I trust, well?

CECILY: Miss Prism has just been complaining of a slight headache. I think it would do her so much good to have a short stroll with you in the park, Dr. Chasuble.

MISS PRISM: [*severely*] Cecily, I have not mentioned anything about a headache.

CECILY: No, dear Miss Prism, I know that, but I felt instinctively that you had a headache. Indeed I was thinking about that, and not about my German lesson, when the Rector came in.

CANON CHASUBLE: I hope, Cecily, you are not inattentive.

CECILY: Oh, I am afraid I am.

CANON CHASUBLE: That is strange. Were I fortunate

enough to be Miss Prism's pupil, I would hang upon her lips. (*Miss Prism glares.*) I spoke metaphorically.—My metaphor was drawn from bees. Ahem! Mr. Worthing, I suppose, has not returned from town yet?

MISS PRISM: We do not expect him till Monday afternoon.

CANON CHASUBLE: Ah, yes, he usually likes to spend his Sunday in London. He is not one of those whose sole aim is enjoyment, as, by all accounts, that unfortunate young man, his brother, seems to be. But I must not disturb Egeria[2] and her pupil any longer.

MISS PRISM: Egeria? My name is Laetitia,[3] Doctor.

CANON CHASUBLE: (*bowing*) A classical allusion merely, drawn from the Pagan authors. I shall see you both no doubt at Evensong.[4]

MISS PRISM: I think, dear Doctor, I will have a stroll with you. I find I have a headache after all, and a walk might do it good.

CANON CHASUBLE: With pleasure, Miss Prism, with pleasure. We might go as far as the schools and back.

MISS PRISM: That would be delightful. Cecily, you will read your Political Economy in my absence. The chapter on the Fall of the Rupee[5] you may omit. It is somewhat too sensational. Even these metallic problems have their melodramatic side. (*She goes down the garden with Dr. Chasuble.*)

CECILY: (*picking up the books and throwing them back on the table*) Horrid Political Economy! Horrid Geography! Horrid, horrid German!

Merriman [*the butler*] *enters with a card on a salver.*

MERRIMAN: Mr. Ernest Worthing has just driven over from the station. He has brought his luggage with him.

CECILY: (*taking the card and reading it*) "Mr. Ernest Worthing, B 4, The Albany, W." Uncle Jack's brother! Did you tell him Mr. Worthing was in town?

---

[2] A legendary Roman nymph who gave counsel to King Numa.
[3] Latin for "happiness."
[4] Evening service of the Anglican Church.
[5] The standard monetary unit of British India.

I think, dear Doctor, I will have a stroll with you.

MERRIMAN: Yes, Miss. He seemed very much disappointed. I mentioned that you and Miss Prism were in the garden. He said he was anxious to speak to you privately for a moment.

CECILY: Ask Mr. Ernest Worthing to come here. I suppose you had better talk to the housekeeper about a room for him.

MERRIMAN: Yes, Miss. (*He goes off.*)

CECILY: I have never met any really wicked person before. I feel rather frightened. I am so afraid he will look just like everyone else.

Algernon enters, very gay and debonair. [*Jaunty straw hat, striking blazer, white flannels, socks, and Oxfords comprise the correct summer costume for a young man in the country.*]

CECILY: [*flatly*] He does!

ALGERNON: (*raising his hat*) You are my little cousin Cecily, I'm sure.

CECILY: [*examining him gravely*] You are under some strange mistake. I am not little. In fact, I am more than usually tall for my age. (*Algernon is rather taken aback.*) But I am your cousin Cecily. You, I see from your card, are Uncle Jack's brother, my cousin Ernest, my wicked cousin Ernest.

ALGERNON: Oh! I am not really wicked at all, cousin Cecily. You mustn't think that I am wicked.

CECILY: [*in solemn moral disapproval*] If you are not, then you have certainly been deceiving us all in a very inexcusable manner. I hope you have not been leading a double life, pretending to be wicked and being really good all the time. That would be hypocrisy.

ALGERNON: (*looking at her in amazement*) Oh! of course I have been rather reckless.

CECILY: I am glad to hear it.

ALGERNON: [*glimpsing the right approach*] In fact, now you mention the subject, I have been very bad in my own small way.

CECILY: I don't think you should be so proud of that, though I am sure it must have been very pleasant.

ALGERNON: It is much pleasanter being here with you.

CECILY: I can't understand how you are here at all. Uncle Jack won't be back till Monday afternoon.

ALGERNON: That is a great disappointment. I am obliged to go up by the first train on Monday morning. I have a business appointment that I am anxious . . . to miss.

CECILY: Couldn't you miss it anywhere but in London?

ALGERNON: No; the appointment is in London.

CECILY: Well, I know, of course, how important it is not to keep a business engagement, if one wants to retain any sense of the beauty of life, but still I think you had better wait till Uncle Jack arrives. I know he wants to speak to you about your emigrating.

ALGERNON: About my what?

CECILY: Your emigrating. He has gone up to buy your outfit.

ALGERNON: I certainly wouldn't let Jack buy my outfit He has no taste in neckties at all.

CECILY: I don't think you will require neckties. Uncle Jack is sending you to Australia.

ALGERNON: [*with infinite disgust*] Australia! I'd sooner die.

CECILY: Well, he said at dinner on Wednesday night, that you would have to choose between this world, the next world, and Australia.

ALGERNON: Oh, well! The accounts I have received of Australia and the next world are not particularly encouraging. This world is good enough for me, cousin Cecily.

CECILY: Yes, but are you good enough for it?

ALGERNON: [*sighing*] I'm afraid I'm not that. [*with great gravity*] That is why I want you to reform me. You might make that your mission, if you don't mind, cousin Cecily.

CECILY: I'm afraid I've not time, this afternoon.

ALGERNON: Well, would you mind my reforming myself this afternoon?

CECILY: That is rather Quixotic of you. But I think you should try.

ALGERNON: I will. I feel better already.

CECILY: You are looking a little worse.

ALGERNON: That is because I am hungry.

CECILY: How thoughtless of me. I should have remembered that when one is going to lead an entirely new life, one requires regular and wholesome meals. Won't you come in?

ALGERNON: Thank you. Might I have a button-hole first? I never have any appetite unless I have a button-hole first.

CECILY: A Marechal Niel?[6] (*picks up scissors*)

ALGERNON: No, I'd sooner have a pink rose.

CECILY: Why? (*cuts a flower*)

ALGERNON: Because you are like a pink rose, cousin Cecily.

CECILY: [*factually*] I don't think it can be right for you to talk to me like that. Miss Prism never says such things to me.

ALGERNON: Then Miss Prism is a short-sighted old lady. (*Cecily puts the rose in his button-hole.*) You are the prettiest girl I ever saw.

CECILY: [*as if merely giving information*] Miss Prism says that all good looks are a snare.

ALGERNON: They are a snare that every sensible man would like to be caught in.

CECILY: [*lightly*] Oh! I don't think I would care to catch a sensible man. I shouldn't know what to talk to him about.

They pass into the house. Miss Prism and Dr. Chasuble return.

MISS PRISM: [*with tender solicitude*] You are too much alone, dear Dr. Chasuble. You should get married. A misanthrope I can understand—a womanthrope, never!

CANON CHASUBLE: (*with a scholar's shudder*) Believe me, I do not deserve so neologistic a phrase. The precept

---

[6] A fragrant, large, golden yellow rose.

as well as the practice of the Primitive Church[7] was distinctly against matrimony.

MISS PRISM: (*sententiously*) That is obviously the reason why the Primitive Church has not lasted up to the present day. And you do not seem to realize, dear Doctor, that by persistently remaining single, a man converts himself into a permanent public temptation. Men should be careful; this very celibacy[8] leads weaker vessels astray.

CANON CHASUBLE: [*vaguely with slow wonderment*] But is a man not equally attractive when married?

MISS PRISM: [*crisply*] No married man is ever attractive except to his wife.

CANON CHASUBLE: [*in gentle sadness*] And often, I've been told, not even to her.

MISS PRISM: [*with aggressive pride*] That depends on the intellectual sympathies of the woman. Maturity can always be depended on. Ripeness can be trusted. Young women are green. (*Dr. Chasuble starts.*) I spoke horticulturally. My metaphor was drawn from fruits. But where is Cecily?

CANON CHASUBLE: Perhaps she followed us to the schools.

Jack enters slowly from the back of the garden. He is dressed in the deepest mourning, with crepe hatband and black gloves. [In this celebrated "mourning scene" Worthing enters with the elegiac gravity and dignified solemnity of a Hamlet just returning from his father's funeral. In black silk top-hat, formal morning coat, striped trousers, patent-leather shoes with dove-grey spats, an elegant, tightly-rolled umbrella, he is the picture

---

[7] A somewhat indefinite term much in favor with the High Church revivalists of the Victorian era. It indicated the Church of the early centuries of the Christian period, especially before the division between the East and the West, the Greek and the Latin. It was felt to be "purer" in creed, doctrine, and practice than the Churches of the Medieval and Reformation periods.

[8] Originally a vow of chastity required of all clerical candidates for the priesthood; abolished in the Church of England at the time of Henry VIII; at the time of Dr. Chasuble, such a practice was entirely voluntary and personal.

of fastidiously tailored grief. It is a part of the stage tradition that he wears in the breast-pocket of his coat a black-edged white silk handkerchief, which he once or twice removes with a gesture of exquisite feeling. He enters back center-stage, standing there sublimely innocent of the presence in the house of the wicked brother Ernest, never so much alive as now that he is being mourned with such dignified gravity. The John Gielgud production stressed the delightful farcicality of the scene by sounding the chimes of a church clock to announce his entrance.]

MISS PRISM: [*startled*] Mr. Worthing!

CANON CHASUBLE: [*in gentle inquiry*] Mr. Worthing?

MISS PRISM: This is indeed a surprise. We did not look for you till Monday afternoon.

JACK: (*shaking Miss Prism's hand in a tragic manner*) I have returned sooner than I expected. Dr. Chasuble, I hope you are well?

CANON CHASUBLE: [*with abstracted solicitude*] Dear Mr. Worthing, I trust this garb of woe does not betoken some terrible calamity?

JACK: [*with resignation*] My brother.

MISS PRISM: [*righteously*] More shameful debts and extravagance?

CANON CHASUBLE: [*with only the vaguest professional interest*] Still leading his life of pleasure?

JACK: [*shaking his head and attempting to cover with the handkerchief a simulated convulsive movement of the throat and tremor of the lower lip and chin as though the agonized memory of so tragic a loss was too great a burden for so tender a heart*] Dead!

CANON CHASUBLE: Your brother Ernest dead?

JACK: [*again as if barely mastering a sudden tidal wave of grief*] Quite dead.

MISS PRISM: [*crisply and with stern satisfaction*] What a lesson for him! I trust he will profit by it.

CANON CHASUBLE: [*with appropriate solemnity*] Mr. Worthing, I offer you my sincere condolence. You have at least the consolation of knowing that you were always the most generous and forgiving of brothers.

JACK: [*with a prodigious sigh*] Poor Ernest! He had many faults, but it is a sad, sad blow.

CANON CHASUBLE: [*sympathetically*] Very sad indeed. Were you with him at the end?

JACK: No. He died abroad; in Paris, in fact. I had a telegram last night from the manager of the Grand Hotel.[9]

CANON CHASUBLE: Was the cause of death mentioned?

JACK: A severe chill, it seems.

MISS PRISM: As a man sows, so shall he reap.

CANON CHASUBLE: (*raising his hand*) Charity, dear Miss Prism, charity! None of us are perfect. I myself am peculiarly susceptible to draughts. Will the interment take place here?

JACK: No. He seems to have expressed a desire to be buried in Paris.

CANON CHASUBLE: In Paris! (*shaking his head*) I fear that hardly points to any very serious state of mind at the last. You would no doubt wish me to make some slight allusion to this tragic domestic affliction next Sunday. (*Jack presses his hand convulsively.*) My sermon on the meaning of the manna in the wilderness can be adapted to almost any occasion, joyful, or, as in the present case, distressing. (*All sigh.*) I have preached it at harvest celebrations, christenings, confirmations, on days of humiliation and festal days. The last time I delivered it was in the Cathedral, as a charity sermon on behalf of the Society for the Prevention of Discontentment among the Upper Orders. The Bishop, who was present, was much struck by some of the analogies I drew.

JACK: Ah, that reminds me, you mentioned christenings I think, Dr. Chasuble. I suppose you know how to christen all right? (*Dr. Chasuble looks astounded.*) I mean, of course, you are continually christening, aren't you?

MISS PRISM: It is, I regret to say, one of the Rector's more constant duties in this parish. I have often spoken

---

[9] A Parisian hotel opened in the 1860's and one of the largest in Europe.

to the poorer classes on the subject. But they don't seem to know what thrift is.

CANON CHASUBLE: [*approaching the subject with delicate reticence*] But is there any particular infant in whom you are interested, Mr. Worthing? Your brother was, I believe, unmarried, was he not?

JACK: Oh, yes.

MISS PRISM: (*bitterly*) People who live entirely for pleasure usually are.

JACK: But it is not for any child, dear Doctor. I am very fond of children. No! The fact is, I would like to be christened myself, this afternoon, if you have nothing better to do.

CANON CHASUBLE: But surely, Mr. Worthing, you have been christened already?

JACK: I don't remember anything about it.

CANON CHASUBLE: But have you any grave doubts on the subject?

JACK: I certainly intend to have. Of course, I don't know if the thing would bother you in any way, or if you think I am a little too old now.

CANON CHASUBLE: Not at all. The sprinkling, and, indeed, the immersion of adults is a perfectly canonical[10] practice.

JACK: Immersion!

CANON CHASUBLE: You need have no apprehensions. Sprinkling is all that is necessary, or indeed I think advisable. Our weather is so changeable. At what hour would you wish the ceremony performed?

JACK: Oh, I might trot around about five if that would suit you.

CANON CHASUBLE: Perfectly, perfectly! In fact I have two similar ceremonies to perform at that time. A case of twins that occurred recently in one of the outlying cottages on your own estate. Poor Jenkins the carter, a most hard-working man.

JACK: Oh! I don't see much fun in being christened

---

[10] According to the regulations of the Church.

along with other babies. It would be childish. Would half-past five do?

CANON CHASUBLE: Admirably! Admirably! (*He takes out his watch.*) And now, dear Mr. Worthing, I will not intrude any longer into a house of sorrow. I would merely beg you not to be too much bowed down by grief. What seem to us bitter trials at the moment are often blessings in disguise.

MISS PRISM: [*drily*] This seems to me a blessing of an extremely obvious kind.

Cecily enters from the house.

CECILY: Uncle Jack! Oh, I am pleased to see you back. [*with sublimely off-beat bluntness*] But what horrid clothes you have on! Do go and change them.

MISS PRISM: [*in sharp reproof*] Cecily!

CANON CHASUBLE: [*with gentle mournfulness*] My child! my child! (*Cecily goes towards Jack; he kisses her brow in a melancholy manner.*)

CECILY: What is the matter, Uncle Jack? Do look happy! You look as if you had a toothache and I have such a surprise for you. Who do you think is in the dining-room? Your brother!

JACK: [*blankly*] Who?

CECILY: [*bubbling with excitement*] Your brother Ernest. He arrived about half an hour ago.

JACK: [*between annoyance and bewilderment*] What nonsense! I haven't got a brother.

CECILY: [*with sweet and gentle persuasiveness*] Oh, don't say that. However badly he may have behaved to you in the past he is still your brother. I'll tell him to come out. And you will shake hands with him, won't you, Uncle Jack? (*She runs back into the house.*)

CANON CHASUBLE: [*dubiously but automatically saying the correct thing*] These are very joyful tidings.

MISS PRISM: [*bluntly*] After we had all been resigned to his loss, his sudden return seems to me peculiarly distressing.

JACK: [*as if in a daze*] My brother is in the dining-room? I don't know what it all means. I think it is perfectly absurd.

Algernon and Cecily enter hand in hand. They come slowly up to Jack.

JACK: Good heavens! (*motions Algernon away*)

ALGERNON: [*with grave sincerity*] Brother John, I have come down from town to tell you that I am very sorry for all the trouble I have given you, and that I intend to lead a better life in the future. (*Jack glares at him and does not take his hand.*)

CECILY: Uncle Jack, you are not going to refuse your own brother's hand?

JACK: [*icily*] Nothing will induce me to take his hand. I think his coming down here disgraceful. He knows perfectly well why.

CECILY: [*in a wheedling tone*] Uncle Jack, do be nice. There is some good in every one. Ernest has just been telling me about his poor invalid friend, Mr. Bunbury, whom he goes to visit so often. And surely there must be much good in one who is kind to an invalid, and leaves the pleasures of London to sit by a bed of pain.

JACK: Oh, he has been talking about Bunbury, has he?

CECILY: Yes, he has told me all about poor Mr. Bunbury, and his terrible state of health.

JACK: [*angrily*] Bunbury! Well, I won't have him talk to you about Bunbury or about anything else. It is enough to drive one perfectly frantic.

ALGERNON: [*temperately*] Of course I admit that the faults were all on my side. But I must say that I think that Brother John's coldness to me is peculiarly painful. I expected a more enthusiastic welcome, especially considering it is the first time I have come here.

CECILY: [*severely*] Uncle Jack, if you don't shake hands with Ernest I will never forgive you.

JACK: [*taken aback*] Never forgive me?

CECILY: [*in a childish chant*] Never, never, never!

JACK: Well, this is the last time I shall ever do it. (*He shakes hands with Algernon and glares.*)

CANON CHASUBLE: [*with relaxed dreaminess and gentle*

professional approval] It's pleasant, is it not, to see so perfect a reconciliation? I think we might leave the two brothers together.

MISS PRISM: Cecily, you will come with us.

CECILY: [*brimming over with benign satisfaction at having accomplished the reconciliation of the brothers*] Certainly, Miss Prism. My little task of reconciliation is over.

CANON CHASUBLE: [*with mellow unction*] You have done a beautiful action today, dear child.

MISS PRISM: [*flatly*] We must not be premature in our judgments.

CECILY: [*sighing ecstatically*] I feel very happy. (*They all go off.*)

JACK: [*turning vehemently on Algernon*] You young scoundrel, Algy, you must get out of this place as soon as possible. I don't allow any Bunburying here.

Merriman enters.

MERRIMAN: I have put Mr. Ernest's things in the room next to yours, sir. I suppose that is all right?

JACK: What?

MERRIMAN: Mr. Ernest's luggage, sir. I have unpacked it and put it in the room next to your own.

JACK: [*dazedly*] His luggage?

MERRIMAN: Yes, sir. Three portmanteaus, a dressing-case, two hat-boxes, and a large luncheon-basket.

ALGERNON: [*apologetically and with infuriating complacency*] I'm afraid I can't stay more than a week this time.

JACK: [*peremptorily*] Merriman, order the dog-cart at once. Mr. Ernest has been suddenly called back to town.

MERRIMAN: Yes, sir. (*He goes back into the house.*)

ALGERNON: [*easily*] What a fearful liar you are, Jack. I have not been called back to town at all.

JACK: [*with cold precision*] Yes, you have.

ALGERNON: I haven't heard any one call me.

JACK: [*conclusively*] Your duty as a gentleman calls you back.

ALGERNON: [*smiling in happy reminiscence*] My duty

as a gentleman has never interfered with my pleasures in the smallest degree.

JACK: [*bitingly*] I can quite understand that.

ALGERNON: [*with genial enthusiasm and as if Jack had not spoken*] Well, Cecily is a darling.

JACK: You are not to talk of Miss Cardew like that. I don't like it.

ALGERNON: [*scrutinizing him carefully*] Well, I don't like your clothes. You look perfectly ridiculous in them. Why on earth don't you go up and change? It is perfectly childish to be in deep mourning for a man who is actually staying for a whole week with you in your house as a guest. I call it grotesque.

JACK: You are certainly not staying with me for a whole week as a guest or anything else. You have got to leave . . . by the four-five train.

ALGERNON: [*briskly and perversely sympathetic*] I certainly won't leave you so long as you are in mourning. It would be most unfriendly. If I were in mourning you would stay with me, I suppose. I should think it very unkind if you didn't.

JACK: Well, will you go if I change my clothes?

ALGERNON: [*thoughtfully*] Yes, if you are not too long. I never saw anybody take so long to dress, and with such little result.

JACK: Well, at any rate, that is better than being always over-dressed as you are.

ALGERNON: If I am occasionally a little over-dressed, I make up for it by being always immensely over-educated.

JACK: Your vanity is ridiculous, your conduct an outrage, and your presence in my garden utterly absurd. However, you have got to catch the four-five, and I hope you will have a pleasant journey back to town. This Bunburying, as you call it, has not been a great success for you. (*He goes into the house.*)

ALGERNON: *I* think it has been a great success. I'm in love with Cecily, and that is everything. (*Cecily enters at the back of the garden. She picks up the can and begins to water the flowers.*) But I must see her before I go, and make arrangements for another Bunbury. Ah, there she is.

CECILY: Oh, I merely came back to water the roses. I thought you were with Uncle Jack.

ALGERNON: [*sombrely*] He's gone to order the dog cart for me.

CECILY: [*delighted*] Oh, is he going to take you for a nice drive?

ALGERNON: [*tragically*] He's going to send me away.

CECILY: [*pouting*] Then have we got to part?

ALGERNON: [*sighing dramatically*] I am afraid so. It's a very painful parting.

CECILY: [*as if repeating a copy-book maxim*] It is always painful to part from people whom one has known for a very brief space of time. The absence of old friends one can endure with equanimity. But even a momentary separation from any one to whom one has just been introduced is almost unbearable.

ALGERNON: [*brightly, with cool politeness*] Thank you.
Merriman enters.

MERRIMAN: The dog-cart is at the door, sir. (*Algernon looks appealingly at Cecily.*)

CECILY: It can wait, Merriman . . . for . . . five minutes.

MERRIMAN: Yes, miss. (*He leaves.*)

ALGERNON: [*with official formality*] I hope, Cecily, I shall not offend you if I state quite frankly and openly that you seem to me to be in every way the visible personification of absolute perfection.

CECILY: [*with equally formal grace*] I think your frankness does you great credit, Ernest. If you will allow me I will copy your remarks into my diary. (*She goes over to the table and begins writing in her diary.*)

ALGERNON: Do you really keep a diary? I'd give anything to look at it. May I?

CECILY: Oh, no. (*putting her hand over it*) You see it is simply a very young girl's record of her own thoughts and impressions, and consequently meant for publication. When it appears in volume form I hope you will order a copy. But pray, Ernest, don't stop. I delight in taking down from dictation. I have reached "absolute perfection." You can go on. I am quite ready for more.

ALGERNON: (*somewhat taken aback*) Ahem! Ahem!

CECILY: [*in delicate mockery of the stiff manner of Miss Prism*] Oh, don't cough, Ernest. When one is dictating one should speak fluently and not cough. Besides, I don't know how to spell a cough. (*She writes as Algernon speaks.*)

ALGERNON: (*speaking very rapidly*) Cecily, ever since I first looked upon your wonderful and incomparable beauty, I have dared to love you wildly, passionately, devotedly, hopelessly.

CECILY: [*with a slight frown*] I don't think that you should tell me that you love me wildly, passionately, devotedly, hopelessly. Hopelessly doesn't seem to make much sense, does it?

ALGERNON: [*ecstatically*] Cecily!

Merriman enters.

MERRIMAN: The dog-cart is waiting, sir.

ALGERNON: Tell it to come round next week, at the same hour.

MERRIMAN: (*looks at Cecily, who makes no sign*) Yes, sir. (*He retires.*)

CECILY: Uncle Jack would be very much annoyed if he knew you were staying on till next week, at the same hour.

ALGERNON: [*impulsively*] Oh, I don't care about Jack. I don't care for anybody in the whole world but you. I love you, Cecily. [*taking her hands*] You will marry me, won't you?

CECILY: You silly you! Of course. Why, we have been engaged for the last three months.

ALGERNON: [*releasing her hands in wonder*] For the last three months?

CECILY: Yes, it will be exactly three months on Thursday.

ALGERNON: But how did we become engaged?

CECILY: Well, ever since dear Uncle Jack first confessed to us that he had a younger brother who was very wicked and bad, you of course have formed the chief topic of conversation between myself and Miss Prism. And of course a man who is much talked about is always very attractive. One feels there must be something in him after all. I dare say it was foolish of me, but I fell in love with you, Ernest.

ALGERNON: Darling! And when was the engagement actually settled?

CECILY: On the fourth of February last. Worn out by your entire ignorance of my existence, I determined to end the matter one way or the other, and after a long struggle with myself I accepted you under this dear old tree here. The next day I bought this little ring in your name, and this is the little bangle with the true lover's knot I promised you always to wear.

ALGERNON: [*regarding the trinket with awe*] Did I give you this? It's very pretty, isn't it?

CECILY: Yes, you've wonderfully good taste, Ernest. It's the excuse I've always given for your leading such a bad life. And this is the box in which I keep all your dear letters. (*She kneels at the table, opens box, and produces letters tied up with blue ribbon.*)

ALGERNON: My letters! But my own sweet Cecily, I have never written you any letters.

CECILY: [*in gentle reproof*] You need hardly remind me of that, Ernest. I remember only too well that I was forced to write your letters for you. I wrote always three times a week, and sometimes oftener.

ALGERNON: Oh, do let me read them, Cecily?

CECILY: Oh, I couldn't possibly. They would make you far too conceited. (*She replaces box.*) The three you wrote me after I had broken off the engagement are so beautiful and so badly spelled, that even now I can hardly read them without crying a little.

ALGERNON: But was our engagement ever broken off?

CECILY: Of course it was. On the 22nd of last March. You can see the entry if you like. (*shows diary*) "Today I broke off my engagement with Ernest. I feel it is better to do so. The weather still continues charming."

ALGERNON: But why on earth did you break it off?

What had I done? I had done nothing at all. Cecily, I am very much hurt indeed to hear you broke it off. Particularly when the weather was so charming.

CECILY: It would hardly have been a really serious engagement if it hadn't been broken off at least once. But I forgave you before the week was out.

ALGERNON: (*crossing to her, and kneeling*) What a perfect angel you are, Cecily.

CECILY: [*with the calm detachment of one reading words from an oculist's chart*] You dear romantic boy. (*He kisses her; she puts her fingers through his hair.*) I hope your hair curls naturally, does it?

ALGERNON: Yes, darling, with a little help from others.

CECILY: I'm so glad.

ALGERNON: [*beseechingly*] You'll never break off our engagement again, Cecily?

CECILY: [*with her usual forthrightness*] I don't think I could break it off now that I have actually met you. Besides, of course, there is the question of your name.

ALGERNON: (*nervously*) Yes, of course.

CECILY: You must not laugh at me, darling, but it had always been a girlish dream of mine to love some one whose name was Ernest. (*Algernon rises, Cecily also.*) There is something in that name that seems to inspire absolute confidence. I pity any poor married woman whose husband is not called Ernest.

ALGERNON: But, my dear child, do you mean to say you could not love me if I had some other name?

CECILY: But what name?

ALGERNON: [*with forced casualness*] Oh, any name you like—Algernon, for instance. . . .

CECILY: But I don't like the name of Algernon.

ALGERNON: Well, my own dear, sweet, loving little darling, I really can't see why you should object to the name of Algernon. It is not at all a bad name. In fact, it is rather an aristocratic name. Half of the chaps who get into the Bankruptcy Court are called Algernon. But seriously, Cecily . . . (*moving to her*) . . . if my name *was* Algy, couldn't you love me?

CECILY: (*rising*) I might respect you, Ernest, I might admire your character, but I fear that I should not be able to give you my undivided attention.

ALGERNON: Ahem! Cecily! (*picking up his hat*) Your Rector here is, I suppose, thoroughly experienced in the practice of all the rites and ceremonials of the church?

CECILY: Oh, yes. Dr. Chasuble is a most learned man. He has never written a single book, so you can imagine how much he knows.

ALGERNON: I must see him at once on a most important christening—I mean on most important business.

CECILY: Oh!

ALGERNON: I sha'n't be away more than half an hour.

CECILY: [*looking hurt*] Considering that we have been engaged since February the 14th, and that I only met you today for the first time, I think it is rather hard that you should leave me for so long a period as half an hour. Couldn't you make it twenty minutes?

ALGERNON: I'll be back in no time. (*He kisses her and rushes down the garden.*)

CECILY: [*thoughtfully*] What an impetuous boy he is. I like his hair so much. I must enter his proposal in my diary.

Merriman enters.

MERRIMAN: A Miss Fairfax has just called to see Mr. Worthing. On very important business, Miss Fairfax states.

CECILY: Isn't Mr. Worthing in his library?

MERRIMAN: Mr. Worthing went over in the direction of the Rectory some time ago.

CECILY: Pray ask the lady to come out here; Mr. Worthing is sure to be back soon. And you can bring tea.

MERRIMAN: Yes, miss. (*He goes out.*)

CECILY: [*musing aloud*] Miss Fairfax! I suppose one of the many good elderly women who are associated with Uncle Jack in some of his philanthropic work in London. I don't quite like women who are interested in philanthropic work. I think it is so forward of them.

Merriman enters.

MERRIMAN: Miss Fairfax.

Gwendolen enters [dressed in most alluring and sophisticated fashionable apparel for an outing in the country.] Merriman retires.

CECILY: (*advancing to meet her*) Pray let me introduce myself to you. My name is Cecily Cardew.

GWENDOLEN: [*eyeing her critically before uttering her name with patronizing condescension*] Cecily Cardew? (*moving to her and shaking hands*) What a very sweet name! Something tells me that we are going to be great friends. I like you already more than I can say. My first impressions of people are never wrong.

CECILY: How nice of you to like me so much after we have known each other such a comparatively short time. Pray sit down.

GWENDOLEN: (*still standing up*) I may call you Cecily, may I not?

CECILY: With pleasure!

GWENDOLEN: [*as if humoring a child*] And you will always call me Gwendolen, won't you?

CECILY: [*noncommittally*] If you wish.

GWENDOLEN: [*with the forced enthusiasm of an adult reaching for the child's confidence*] Then that is all quite settled, is it not?

CECILY: I hope so. (*A pause. They both sit down together.*)

GWENDOLEN: [*with an easy air of conscious superiority*] Perhaps this might be a favorable opportunity for my mentioning who I am. My father is Lord Bracknell. You have never heard of papa, I suppose?

CECILY: I don't think so.

GWENDOLEN: [*patronizingly*] Outside the family circle, papa, I am glad to say, is entirely unknown. I think that is quite as it should be. The home seems to me to be the proper sphere for the man. And certainly once a man begins to neglect his domestic duties he becomes painfully effeminate, does he not? And I don't like that. It makes men so very attractive. Cecily, mamma, whose views on education are remarkably strict, has brought me up to be extremely short-sighted; it is part of her system; so do you mind my looking at you through my glasses? [*raising her lorgnette*]

CECILY: Oh, not at all, Gwendolen. I am very fond of being looked at.

GWENDOLEN: (*after examining Cecily carefully through her lorgnette*) You are here on a short visit, I suppose.

CECILY: Oh, no, I live here.

GWENDOLEN: (*severely*) Really? Your mother, no doubt, or some female relative of advanced years, resides here also?

CECILY: Oh, no. I have no mother, nor, in fact, any relations.

GWENDOLEN: (*with the chill, rising inflections of a woman whose worst suspicions are threatened with confirmation*) Indeed?

CECILY: My dear guardian, with the assistance of Miss Prism, has the arduous task of looking after me.

GWENDOLEN: Your guardian?

CECILY: Yes, I am Mr. Worthing's ward.

GWENDOLEN: [*raising her eyebrows*] Oh! It is strange he never mentioned to me that he had a ward. How secretive of him! He grows more interesting hourly. I am not sure, however, that the news inspires me with feelings of unmixed delight. (*rising and going to her*) I am very fond of you, Cecily; I have liked you ever since I met you. But I am bound to state that now that I know that you are Mr. Worthing's ward, I cannot help expressing a wish you were—well, just a little older than you seem to be—and not quite so very alluring in appearance. In fact, if I may speak candidly—

CECILY: [*simply—but not artlessly*] Pray do! I think that whenever one has anything unpleasant to say, one should always be quite candid.

GWENDOLEN: [*weighing her words*] Well, to speak with perfect candor, Cecily, I wish that you were fully forty-two, and more than usually plain for your age. Ernest has a strong upright nature. He is the very soul of truth and honor. Disloyalty would be as impossible to him as deception. But even men of the noblest possible moral character are extremely susceptible to the influence of the physical charms of others. Modern, no less than Ancient History, supplies us with many most painful examples of what I refer to. If it were not so, indeed, History would be quite unreadable.

CECILY: I beg your pardon, Gwendolen, did you say Ernest?

GWENDOLEN: Yes.

CECILY: Oh, but it is not Mr. Ernest Worthing who is my guardian. It is his brother—his elder brother.

GWENDOLEN: (*sitting down again*) Ernest never mentioned to me that he had a brother.

CECILY: I am sorry to say they have not been on good terms for a long time.

GWENDOLEN: [*relieved*] Ah! that accounts for it. And now that I think of it I have never heard any man mention his brother. The subject seems distasteful to most men. Cecily, you have lifted a load from my mind. I was growing almost anxious. It would have been terrible if any cloud had come across a friendship like ours, would it not? Of course you are quite, quite sure that it is not Mr. Ernest Worthing who is your guardian?

CECILY: Quite sure. (*A pause.*) In fact, I am going to be his.

GWENDOLEN: (*enquiringly*) I beg your pardon?

CECILY: (*rather shy and confidingly*) Dearest Gwendolen, there is no reason why I should make a secret of it to you. Our little county newspaper is sure to chronicle the fact next week. Mr. Ernest Worthing and I are engaged to be married.

GWENDOLEN: (*quite politely, rising*) My darling Cecily, I think there must be some slight error. Mr. Ernest Worthing is engaged to me. The announcement will appear in the *Morning Post*[11] on Saturday at the latest.

CECILY: (*very politely, rising*) I am afraid you must be

---

[11] A London daily which particularly featured society announcements.

under some misconception. Ernest proposed to me exactly ten minutes ago. (*shows her diary*)

GWENDOLEN: (*examining the diary through her lorgnette carefully*) It is certainly very curious, for he asked me to be his wife yesterday afternoon at 5.30. If you would care to verify the incident, pray do so. (*produces diary of her own*) I never travel without my diary. One should always have something sensational to read in the train. I am so sorry, dear Cecily, if it is any disappointment to you, but I'm afraid *I* have the prior claim.

CECILY: [*with kindly solicitude—but served at somewhat less than room temperature*] It would distress me more than I can tell you, dear Gwendolen, if it caused you any mental or physical anguish, but I feel bound to point out that since Ernest proposed to you he clearly has changed his mind.

GWENDOLEN: (*meditatively*) If the poor fellow has been entrapped into any foolish promise I shall consider it my duty to rescue him at once, and with a firm hand.

CECILY: (*thoughtfully and sadly*) Whatever unfortunate entanglement my dear boy may have got into, I will never reproach him with it after we are married.

GWENDOLEN: [*with haughty anger masked in cool contempt*] Do you allude to me, Miss Cardew, as an entanglement? You are presumptuous. On an occasion of this kind it becomes more than a moral duty to speak one's mind. It becomes a pleasure.

CECILY: [*with mounting irritation spiced with provoking politeness*] Do you suggest, Miss Fairfax, that I entrapped Ernest into an engagement? How dare you? This is no time for wearing the shallow mask of manners. When I see a spade I call it a spade.

GWENDOLEN: [*satirically—in a voice as from distant Olympus*] I am glad to say that I have never seen a spade. It is obvious that our social spheres have been widely different.

Merriman enters, followed by the footman. He carries a salver, tablecloth, and plate-stand. Cecily is about to retort. The presence of the servants exercises a restraining influence, under which both girls chafe.

MERRIMAN: Shall I lay tea here as usual, miss?

CECILY: (*sternly, in a calm voice*) Yes, as usual. (*Merriman begins to clear and lay cloth. A long pause. Cecily and Gwendolen glare at each other.*)

GWENDOLEN: Are there many interesting walks in the vicinity, Miss Cardew?

CECILY: Oh, yes, a great many. From the top of one of the hills quite close one can see five counties.

GWENDOLEN: Five counties! I don't think I should like that. I hate crowds.

CECILY: (*sweetly*) I suppose that is why you live in town? (*Gwendolen bites her lip, and beats her foot nervously with her parasol.*)

GWENDOLEN: (*looking around*) Quite a well-kept garden this is, Miss Cardew.

CECILY: [*with artful and decorous indifference*] So glad you like it, Miss Fairfax.

GWENDOLEN: I had no idea there were any flowers in the country.

CECILY: Oh, flowers are as common here, Miss Fairfax, as people are in London.

GWENDOLEN: Personally I cannot understand how anybody manages to exist in the country, if anybody who is anybody does. The country always bores me to death.

CECILY: Ah! This is what the newspapers call agricultural depression, is it not? I believe the aristocracy are suffering very much from it just at present. It is almost an epidemic amongst them, I have been told. May I offer you some tea, Miss Fairfax?

GWENDOLEN: (*with elaborate politeness*) Thank you. (*aside*) Detestable girl! But I require tea!

CECILY: (*sweetly*) Sugar?

GWENDOLEN: (*superciliously*) No thank you. Sugar is not fashionable any more. (*Cecily looks angrily at her, takes up the tongs and puts four lumps of sugar into the cup.*)

CECILY: (*severely*) Cake or bread and butter?

GWENDOLEN: (*in a bored manner*) Bread and butter, please. Cake is rarely seen at the best houses now-a-days.

CECILY: (*cutting a very large slice of cake, and putting it on the tray*) Hand that to Miss Fairfax. (*Merriman does so, and goes out with the footman. Gwendolen drinks the tea and makes a grimace. She puts down her cup at once, reaches out her hand to the bread and butter, looks at it, and finds it is cake. She rises in indignation.*)

GWENDOLEN: [*with a politely restrained note of crisis in her voice*] You have filled my tea with lumps of sugar, and though I asked most distinctly for bread and butter, you have given me cake. I am known for the gentleness of my disposition, and the extraordinary sweetness of my nature, but I warn you, Miss Cardew, you may go too far.

CECILY: (*rising*) To save my poor, innocent, trusting boy from the machinations of any other girl there are no lengths to which I would not go.

GWENDOLEN: [*regarding her distastefully*] From the moment I saw you I distrusted you. I felt that you were false and deceitful. I am never deceived in such matters. My first impressions of people are invariably right.

CECILY: [*with studied politeness*] It seems to me, Miss Fairfax, that I am trespassing on your valuable time. No doubt you have many other calls of a similar character to make in the neighborhood.

Jack enters.

GWENDOLEN: (*catching sight of him*) Ernest! My own Ernest!

JACK: Gwendolen! Darling! (*offers to kiss her*)

GWENDOLEN: (*drawing back*) A moment! May I ask if you are engaged to be married to this young lady? (*pointing to Cecily*)

JACK: (*laughing*) To dear little Cecily! Of course not! What could have put such an idea into your pretty little head?

GWENDOLEN: Thank you. You may. (*offers her cheek*)

CECILY: (*very sweetly*) I knew there must be some misunderstanding, Miss Fairfax. The gentleman whose arm is at present around your waist is my dear guardian, Mr. John Worthing.

GWENDOLEN: I beg your pardon?

CECILY: This is Uncle Jack.

GWENDOLEN: (*receding*) Jack! Oh!

Algernon enters.

CECILY: Here is Ernest.

ALGERNON: (*going straight over to Cecily without noticing anyone else*) My own love! (*offers to kiss her*)

CECILY: (*drawing back*) A moment, Ernest! May I ask you—are you engaged to be married to this young lady?

ALGERNON: (*looking round*) To what young lady? Good heavens! Gwendolen!

CECILY: Yes, to good heavens, Gwendolen; I mean to Gwendolen.

ALGERNON: (*laughing*) Of course not! What could have put such an idea into your pretty little head?

CECILY: Thank you. (*presenting her cheek to be kissed*) You may. (*Algernon kisses her.*)

GWENDOLEN: [*in a voice still edged with condescension*] I felt there was some slight error, Miss Cardew. The gentleman who is now embracing you is my cousin, Mr. Algernon Moncrieff.

CECILY: (*breaking away from Algernon*) Algernon Moncrieff! Oh! (*The two girls move towards each other and put their arms round each other's waists as if for protection.*)

CECILY: Are you called Algernon?

ALGERNON: I cannot deny it.

CECILY: Oh!

GWENDOLEN: Is your name really John?

JACK: (*standing rather proudly*) I could deny it if I liked. I could deny anything if I liked. But my name certainly is John. It has been John for years.

CECILY: (*to Gwendolen*) A gross deception has been practiced on both of us.

GWENDOLEN: My poor wounded Cecily!

CECILY: My sweet, wronged Gwendolen!

GWENDOLEN: (*slowly and seriously*) You will call me sister, will you not? (*They embrace. Jack and Algernon groan and walk up and down.*)

CECILY: (*rather brightly*) There is just one question I would like to be allowed to ask my guardian.

GWENDOLEN: An admirable idea! Mr. Worthing, there is just one question I would like to be permitted to put to you. Where is your brother Ernest? We are both engaged to be married to your brother Ernest, so it is a matter of some importance to us to know where your brother Ernest is at present.

JACK: (*slowly and hesitatingly*) Gwendolen—Cecily—it is very painful for me to be forced to speak the truth. It is the first time in my life that I have ever been reduced to such a painful position, and I am really quite inexperienced in doing anything of the kind. However, I will tell you quite frankly that I have no brother Ernest. I have no brother at all. I never had a brother in my life, and I certainly have not the smallest intention of ever having one in the future.

CECILY: (*surprised*) No brother at all?

JACK: (*cheerily*) None!

GWENDOLEN: (*severely*) Had you never a brother of any kind?

JACK: (*pleasantly*) Never. Not even of any kind.

GWENDOLEN: [*ruefully*] I am afraid it is quite clear, Cecily, that neither of us is engaged to be married to any one.

CECILY: It is not a very pleasant position for a young girl suddenly to find herself in. Is it?

GWENDOLEN: Let us go into the house. They will hardly venture to come after us there.

CECILY: No, men are so cowardly, aren't they. (*They retire into the house with scornful looks.*)

JACK: [*coldly*] This ghastly state of things is what you call Bunburying, I suppose?

ALGERNON: [*enthusiastically*] Yes, and a perfectly wonderful Bunbury it is. The most wonderful Bunbury I have ever had in my life.

JACK: [*sharply*] Well, you've no right whatsoever to Bunbury here.

ALGERNON: [*reasonably*] That is absurd. One has a right to Bunbury anywhere one chooses. Every serious Bunburyist knows that.

JACK: Serious Bunburyist! Good heavens!

ALGERNON: Well, one must be serious about something, if one wants to have any amusement in life. I happen to be serious about Bunburying. What on earth you are serious about I haven't got the remotest idea. About everything, I should fancy. You have such an absolutely trivial nature.

JACK: Well, the only small satisfaction I have in the whole of this wretched business is that your friend Bunbury is quite exploded. You won't be able to run down to the country quite so often as you used to do, dear Algy. And a very good thing, too.

ALGERNON: Your brother is a little off color, isn't he, dear Jack? You won't be able to disappear to London quite so frequently as your wicked custom was. And not a bad thing either.

JACK: [*in his best pulpit manner*] As for your conduct towards Miss Cardew, I must say that your taking in a sweet, simple, innocent girl like that is quite inexcusable. To say nothing of the fact that she is my ward.

ALGERNON: [*deliberately mimicking Jack*] I can see no possible defense at all for your deceiving a brilliant, clever, thoroughly experienced young lady like Miss Fairfax. To say nothing of the fact that she is my cousin.

JACK: [*as though speaking out of a more transparently pure nature*] I wanted to be engaged to Gwendolen, that is all. I love her.

ALGERNON: Well, I simply wanted to be engaged to Cecily. I adore her.

JACK: There is certainly no chance of your marrying Miss Cardew.

ALGERNON: I don't think there is much likelihood, Jack, of you and Miss Fairfax being united.

JACK: Well, that is no business of yours.

ALGERNON: If it was my business, I wouldn't talk about it. (*begins to eat muffins*) It is very vulgar to talk about one's business. Only people like stock-brokers do that, and then merely at dinner parties.

[*In this scene, Algy and Jack behave with a carefully disciplined greediness in which food is consumed as rapidly as perfect decorum will allow; their bearing towards each other is stiffly reserved and finely edged with a pointed and poisonous politeness—another specimen of the Gwendolen-Cecily tiff at tea-service.*]

JACK: How you can sit there, calmly eating muffins, when we are in this horrible trouble, I can't make out. You seem to me to be perfectly heartless.

ALGERNON: Well, I can't eat muffins in an agitated manner. The butter would probably get on my cuffs. One should always eat muffins quite calmly. It is the only way to eat them.

JACK: I say it's perfectly heartless your eating muffins at all, under the circumstances.

ALGERNON: [*devouring his muffins with ferocious calmness*] When I am in trouble, eating is the only thing that consoles me. Indeed, when I am in really great trouble, as any one who knows me intimately will tell you, I refuse everything except food and drink. At the present moment I am eating muffins because I am unhappy. Besides, I am particularly fond of muffins. (*rising*)

JACK: (*rising*) Well, that is no reason why you should eat them all in that greedy way. (*takes muffins from Algernon*)

ALGERNON: (*offering tea-cake*) I wish you would have tea-cake instead. I don't like tea-cake.

JACK: Good heavens! I suppose a man may eat his own muffins in his own garden.

ALGERNON: But you have just said it was perfectly heartless to eat muffins.

JACK: I said it was perfectly heartless of you, under the circumstances. That is a very different thing.

ALGERNON: That may be. But the muffins are the same. (*He seizes the muffin-dish from Jack.*)

JACK: Algy, I wish to goodness you would go.

ALGERNON: You can't possibly ask me to go without having some dinner. It's absurd. I never go without my dinner. No one ever does, except vegetarians and people like that. Besides I have just made arrangements with Dr. Chasuble to be christened at a quarter to six under the name of Ernest.

JACK: My dear fellow, the sooner you give up that nonsense the better. I made arrangements this morning with Dr. Chasuble to be christened myself at 5:30, and I naturally will take the name of Ernest. Gwendolen would wish it. We can't both be christened Ernest. It's absurd. Besides, I have a perfect right to be christened if I like. There is no evidence at all that I ever have been christened by anybody. I should think it extremely probable I never was, and so does Dr. Chasuble. It is entirely different in your case. You have been christened already.

ALGERNON: Yes, but I have not been christened for years.

JACK: Yes, but you *have* been christened. That is the important thing.

ALGERNON: Quite so. So I know my constitution can stand it. If you are not quite sure about your ever having been christened, I must say I think it rather dangerous your venturing on it now. It might make you very unwell. You can hardly have forgotten that some one very closely connected with you was very nearly carried off this week in Paris by a severe chill.

JACK: Yes, but you said yourself that a severe chill was not hereditary.

ALGERNON: It usedn't to be, I know—but I daresay it is now. Science is always making wonderful improvements in things.

JACK: (*picking up the muffin-dish*) Oh, that is nonsense, you are always talking nonsense.

ALGERNON: Jack, you are at the muffins again! I wish you wouldn't. There are only two left. (*takes them*) I told you I was particularly fond of muffins.

JACK: But I hate tea-cake.

ALGERNON: Why on earth then do you allow tea-cake to be served up for you guests? What ideas you have of hospitality!

JACK: Algernon! I have already told you to go. I don't want you here. Why don't you go?

ALGERNON: I haven't quite finished my tea yet, and there is still one muffin left. (*Jack groans, and sinks into a chair. Algernon still continues eating.*)

CURTAIN

ACT THREE

Morning-room at the Manor House. [A typical Victorian high-ceilinged room with large-patterned wallpaper and a proliferation of hangings and potted plants. It is over-furnished with sofa, secretary, occasional chairs, and tables. A tall window is centered in the back wall, to the right of which is a built-in bookcase, full of leather-covered volumes and matched sets.] Gwendolen and Cecily are at the window looking out into the garden. [A portal at the left between the windows and the front of the stage leads to the hall. A door at the right leads to other rooms on the ground floor.]

GWENDOLEN: [*with disappointment*] The fact that they did not follow us at once into the house, as any one else would have done, seems to me to show that they have some sense of shame left.

CECILY: [*bitterly*] They have been eating muffins. That looks like repentance.

GWENDOLEN: (*after a pause*) They don't seem to notice us at all. Couldn't you cough? [*Cecily obliges.*]

GWENDOLEN: [*pleased*] They're looking at us. What effrontery!

CECILY: [*excitedly*] They're approaching. That's very forward of them.

GWENDOLEN: Let us preserve a dignified silence.

CECILY: Certainly. It's the only thing to do.

Jack enters, followed by Algernon. They whistle some dreadful popular air from a British opera.

128

GWENDOLEN: [*in disgust*] This dignified silence seems to produce an unpleasant effect.

CECILY: A most distasteful one.

GWENDOLEN: But we will not be the first to speak.

CECILY: Certainly not.

GWENDOLEN: [*solemnly*] Mr. Worthing, I have something very particular to ask you. Much depends on your reply.

CECILY: Gwendolen, your common sense is invaluable. Mr. Moncrieff, kindly answer me the following question. Why did you pretend to be my guardian's brother?

ALGERNON: In order that I might have an opportunity of meeting you.

CECILY: (*to Gwendolen*) That certainly seems a satisfactory explanation, does it not?

GWENDOLEN: [*tartly*] Yes, dear, if you can believe him.

CECILY: I don't. But that does not affect the wonderful beauty of his answer.

GWENDOLEN: True. In matters of grave importance, style, not sincerity, is the vital thing. Mr. Worthing, what explanation can you offer to me for pretending to have a brother? Was it in order that you might have an opportunity of coming up to town to see me as often as possible?

JACK: [*ardently*] Can you doubt it, Miss Fairfax?

GWENDOLEN: I have the gravest doubts upon the subject. But I intend to crush them. This is not the moment for German skepticism.[1] (*moving to Cecily*) Their explanations appear to be quite satisfactory, especially Mr. Worthing's. That seems to me to have the stamp of truth upon it.

CECILY: I am more than content with what Mr. Moncrieff said. His voice alone inspires one with absolute credulity.

GWENDOLEN: Then you think we should forgive them?

---

[1] Referring especially to the Higher Criticism of the Bible, a microscopic method of analysis which tended to throw doubt upon the authenticity and reliability of various books of the Old and New Testaments.

CECILY: [*hastily*] Yes, I mean no.

GWENDOLEN: True! I had forgotten. There are principles at stake that one cannot surrender. Which of us should tell them? The task is not a pleasant one.

CECILY: Could we not both speak at the same time?

GWENDOLEN: An excellent idea! I nearly always speak at the same time as other people. Will you take the time from me?

CECILY: Certainly. (*Gwendolen beats time with uplifted finger.*)

GWENDOLEN and CECILY: (*speaking together*) Your Christian names are still an insuperable barrier. That is all!

JACK and ALGERNON: (*speaking together*) Our Christian names! Is that all? But we are going to be christened this afternoon.

GWENDOLEN: (*to Jack*) For my sake you are prepared to do this terrible thing?

JACK: [*solemnly*] I am.

CECILY: (*to Algernon*) To please me you are ready to face this fearful ordeal?

ALGERNON: [*heroically*] I am!

GWENDOLEN: [*sighing in awe and wonder*] How absurd to talk of the equality of the sexes! Where questions of self-sacrifice are concerned, men are infinitely beyond us.

JACK: [*with simple modesty*] We are. (*clasps hands with Algernon*)

CECILY: [*lost in admiration*] They have moments of physical courage of which we women know absolutely nothing.

GWENDOLEN: (*to Jack*) Darling!

ALGERNON: (*to Cecily*) Darling! (*They fall into each other's arms.*)

Merriman enters. When he enters he coughs loudly, seeing the situation.

MERRIMAN: Ahem! Ahem! Lady Bracknell!

JACK: Good heavens!

Lady Bracknell enters. The couples separate in alarm. Merriman leaves.

LADY BRACKNELL: [*with the utmost severity*] Gwendolen! What does this mean?

GWENDOLEN: [*with respectful resoluteness*] Merely that I am engaged to be married to Mr. Worthing, Mamma.

LADY BRACKNELL: [*entirely unaffected by the revelation and continuing with an air of authority expressed in oracular manner*] Come here. Sit down. Sit down immediately. Hesitation is a sign of mental decay in the young, of physical weakness in the old. (*turning to Jack*) Apprised, sir, of my daughter's sudden flight by her trusty maid, whose confidence I purchased by means of a small coin, I followed her at once by a luggage train. Her unhappy father is, I am glad to say, under the impression that she is attending a more than usually lengthy lecture by the University Extension Scheme on the Influence of a Permanent Income on Thought. I do not propose to undeceive him. Indeed I have never undeceived him on any question. I would consider it wrong. But of course you will clearly understand that all communication between yourself and my daughter must cease immediately from this moment. On this point, as indeed on all points, I am firm.

JACK: [*bravely*] I am engaged to be married to Gwendolen, Lady Bracknell!

LADY BRACKNELL: [*casually*] You are nothing of the kind, sir. And now, as regards Algernon! . . . Algernon!

ALGERNON: [*rigidly respectful*] Yes, Aunt Augusta.

LADY BRACKNELL: May I ask if it is in this house that your invalid friend Mr. Bunbury resides?

ALGERNON: (*stammering*) Oh, no! Bunbury doesn't live here. Bunbury is somewhere else at present. In fact, Bunbury is dead.

LADY BRACKNELL: [*in deprecatory surprise as if anyone could dare take so decisive a step without consulting her*] Dead! When did Mr. Bunbury die? His death must have been extremely sudden.

ALGERNON: (*airily*) Oh, I killed Bunbury this afternoon. I mean poor Bunbury died this afternoon.

LADY BRACKNELL: [*severely*] What did he die of?

ALGERNON: [*vaguely*] Bunbury? Oh, he was quite exploded.

LADY BRACKNELL: [*with righteous indignation*] Exploded! Was he the victim of a revolutionary outrage? I was not aware that Mr. Bunbury was interested in social legislation. If so, he is well punished for his morbidity.

ALGERNON: [*placatingly*] My dear Aunt Augusta, I mean he was found out! The doctors found out that Bunbury could not live, that is what I mean—so Bunbury died.

LADY BRACKNELL: [*with great definiteness*] He seems to have had great confidence in the opinion of his physicians. I am glad, however, that he made up his mind at the last to some definite course of action, and acted under proper medical advice. And now that we have finally got rid of this Mr. Bunbury, may I ask, Mr. Worthing, who is that young person whose hand my nephew Algernon is now holding in what seems to me a peculiarly unnecessary manner?

JACK: That lady is Miss Cecily Cardew, my ward. (*Lady Bracknell bows coldly to Cecily.*)

ALGERNON: [*quietly*] I am engaged to be married to Cecily, Aunt Augusta.

LADY BRACKNELL: [*as if not having heard him*] I beg your pardon?

CECILY: [*with crystal-clear accents*] Mr. Moncrieff and I are engaged to be married, Lady Bracknell.

LADY BRACKNELL: (*with a shiver, crossing to the sofa and sitting down*) I do not know whether there is anything peculiarly exciting in the air of this particular part of Hertfordshire, but the number of engagements that go on seems to me considerably above the proper average that statistics have laid down for our guidance. I think some preliminary enquiry on my part would not be out of place. [*with her most annihilating glare*] Mr. Worthing, is Miss Cardew at all connected with any of the larger railway stations in London? I merely desire information.

Until yesterday I had no idea that there were any families or persons whose origin was a Terminus. (*Jack looks perfectly furious, but restrains himself.*)

JACK: (*in a clear, cold voice*) Miss Cardew is the granddaughter of the late Mr. Thomas Cardew of 149 Belgrave Square, S. W.; Gervase Park, Dorking, Surrey; and the Sporan, Fifeshire, N.B.[2]

LADY BRACKNELL: [*meditatively*] That sounds not unsatisfactory. Three addresses always inspire confidence, even in tradesmen. But what proof have I of their authenticity?

JACK: I have carefully preserved the Court Guide[3] of the period. They are open to your inspection, Lady Bracknell.

LADY BRACKNELL: (*grimly*) I have known strange errors in that publication.

JACK: Miss Cardew's family solicitors are Messrs. Markby, Markby, and Markby.

LADY BRACKNELL: [*repeating, as if the incantatory rhythm had hypnotized her*] Markby, Markby, and Markby? A firm of the very highest position in their profession. Indeed I am told that one of the Mr. Markbys is occasionally to be seen at dinner parties. So far I am satisfied.

JACK: (*very irritably*) How extremely kind of you, Lady Bracknell! I have also in my possession, you will be pleased to hear, certificates of Miss Cardew's birth, baptism, whooping cough, registration, vaccination, confirmation, and the measles; both the German and the English variety.

LADY BRACKNELL: Ah! A life crowded with incident, I see; though perhaps somewhat too exciting for a young girl. I am not myself in favor of premature experiences. (*She rises, looks at her watch.*) Gwendolen! the time approaches for our departure. We have not a moment to

---

[2] N.B.—North Britain, Scotland.

[3] Court Guides give a detailed account of titled worthies in Church and State.

lose. As a matter of form, Mr. Worthing, I had better ask you if Miss Cardew has any little fortune?

JACK: [*with malicious casualness*] Oh, about a hundred and thirty thousand pounds in the Funds.[4] That is all. Good-by, Lady Bracknell. So pleased to have seen you.

LADY BRACKNELL: (*sitting down again*) A moment, Mr. Worthing. A hundred and thirty thousand pounds! And in the Funds! Miss Cardew seems to be a most attractive young lady, now that I look at her. Few girls of the present day have any really solid qualities, any of the qualities that last, and improve with time. We live, I regret to say, in an age of surfaces. (*to Cecily*) Come over here, dear. (*Cecily goes across.*) Pretty child! your dress is sadly simple, and your hair seems almost as Nature might have left it. But we can soon alter all that. A thoroughly experienced French maid produces a really marvellous result in a very brief space of time. I remember recommending one to young Lady Lancing, and after three months her own husband did not know her.

JACK: (*aside*) And after six months nobody knew her.

LADY BRACKNELL: (*glares at Jack for a few moments. Then bends, with a practiced smile, to Cecily*) Kindly turn round, sweet child. (*Cecily turns completely round.*) No, the side view is what I want. (*Cecily presents her profile.*) Yes, quite as I expected. There are distinct social possibilities in your profile. The two weak points in our age are its want of principle and its want of profile. The chin a little higher, dear. Style largely depends on the way the chin is worn. They are worn very high, just at present. Algernon!

ALGERNON: Yes, Aunt Augusta!

LADY BRACKNELL: There are distinct social possibilities in Miss Cardew's profile.

ALGERNON: [*impetuously*] Cecily is the sweetest, dearest, prettiest girl in the whole world. And I don't care twopence about social possibilities.

---

[4] British government bonds.

LADY BRACKNELL: [*coldly*] Never speak disrespectfully of society, Algernon. Only people who can't get into it do that. (*to Cecily*) Dear child, of course you know that Algernon has nothing but his debts to depend upon. But I do not approve of mercenary marriages. When I married Lord Bracknell I had no fortune of any kind. But I never dreamed for a moment of allowing that to stand in my way. Well, I suppose I must give my consent.

ALGERNON: [*humbly*] Thank you, Aunt Augusta.

LADY BRACKNELL: [*graciously*] Cecily, you may kiss me!

CECILY: (*kissing her*) Thank you, Lady Bracknell.

LADY BRACKNELL: [*in a tone softened by the impact of £130,000*] You may also address me as Aunt Augusta for the future.

CECILY: Thank you, Aunt Augusta.

LADY BRACKNELL: The marriage, I think, had better take place quite soon.

ALGERNON: Thank you, Aunt Augusta.

CECILY: Thank you, Aunt Augusta.

LADY BRACKNELL: To speak frankly, I am not in favor of long engagements. They give people the opportunity of finding out each other's character before marriage, which I think is never advisable.

JACK: I beg your pardon for interrupting you, Lady Bracknell, but his engagement is quite out of the question. I am Miss Cardew's guardian, and she cannot marry without my consent until she comes of age. That consent I absolutely decline to give.

LADY BRACKNELL: Upon what grounds, may I ask? Algernon is an extremely, I may almost say an ostentatiously eligible young man. He has nothing, but he looks everything. What more can one desire?

JACK: It pains me very much to have to speak frankly to you, Lady Bracknell, about your nephew, but the fact is that I do not approve at all of his moral character. I suspect him of being untruthful. (*Algernon and Cecily look at him in indignant amazement.*)

LADY BRACKNELL: Untruthful! My nephew Algernon? Impossible! He is an Oxonian.

JACK: I fear there can be no possible doubt about the matter. This afternoon, during my temporary absence in London on an important question of romance, he obtained admission to my house by means of the false pretense of being my brother. Under an assumed name he drank, I've just been informed by my butler, an entire pint bottle of my Perrier-Jouet, Brut, '89;[5] a wine I was specially reserving for myself. Continuing his disgraceful deception, he succeeded in the course of the afternoon in alienating the affections of my only ward. He subsequently stayed to tea, and devoured every single muffin. And what makes his conduct all the more heartless is, that he was perfectly well aware from the first that I have no brother, that I never had a brother, and that I don't intend to have a brother, not even of any kind. I distinctly told him so myself yesterday afternoon.

LADY BRACKNELL: [*judiciously*] Ahem! Mr. Worthing, after careful consideration I have decided entirely to overlook my nephew's conduct to you.

JACK: That is very generous of you, Lady Bracknell. My own decision, however, is unalterable. I decline to give my consent.

LADY BRACKNELL: (*to Cecily*) Come here, sweet child. (*Cecily goes over.*) How old are you, dear?

CECILY: Well, I am really only eighteen, but I always admit to twenty when I go to evening parties.

LADY BRACKNELL: You are perfectly right in making some slight alteration. Indeed, no woman should ever be quite accurate about her age. It looks so calculating. . . . (*in a meditative manner*) Eighteen, but admitting to twenty at evening parties. Well, it will not be very long before you are of age and free from restraints of tutelage. So I don't think your guardian's consent is, after all, a matter of any importance.

JACK: Pray excuse me, Lady Bracknell, for interrupting

---

[5] An especially dry vintage champagne of that year.

you again, but it is only fair to tell you that according to the terms of her grandfather's will Miss Cardew does not come legally of age till she is thirty-five.

LADY BRACKNELL: That does not seem to me to be a grave objection. Thirty-five is a very attractive age. London society is full of women of the very highest birth who have, of their own free choice, remained thirty-five for years. Lady Dumbleton is an instance in point. To my knowledge she has been thirty-five ever since she arrived at the age of forty, which was many years ago. I see no reason why our dear Cecily should not be even still more attractive at the age you mention than she is at present. There will be a large accumulation of property.

CECILY: Algy, could you wait for me till I was thirty-five?

ALGERNON: Of course I could, Cecily. You know I could.

CECILY: Yes, I felt it instinctively, but I couldn't wait all that time. I hate waiting even five minutes for anybody. It always makes me rather cross. I am not punctual myself, I know, but I do like punctuality in others, and waiting, even to be married, is quite out of the question.

ALGERNON: Then what is to be done, Cecily?

CECILY: [*distantly*] I don't know, Mr. Moncrieff.

LADY BRACKNELL: [*brightly*] My dear Mr. Worthing, as Miss Cardew states positively that she cannot wait till she is thirty-five—a remark which I am bound to say seems to show a somewhat impatient nature—I would beg of you to reconsider your decision.

JACK: But, my dear Lady Bracknell, the matter is entirely in your own hands. The moment you consent to my marriage with Gwendolen, I will most gladly allow your nephew to form an alliance with my ward.

LADY BRACKNELL: (*rising and drawing herself up*) You must be quite aware that what you propose is out of the question.

JACK: Then a passionate celibacy is all that any of us can look forward to.

LADY BRACKNELL: [*firmly*] That is not the destiny I

propose for Gwendolen. Algernon, of course, can choose for himself. (*pulls out her watch*) Come, dear (*Gwendolen rises*), we have already missed five, if not six, trains. To miss any more might expose us to comment on the platform.

Dr. Chasuble enters.

CANON CHASUBLE: Everything is quite ready for the christenings.

LADY BRACKNELL: The christenings, sir! Is not that somewhat premature?

CANON CHASUBLE: (*looking rather puzzled, and pointing to Jack and Algernon*) Both these gentlemen have expressed a desire for immediate baptism.

LADY BRACKNELL: At their age? The idea is grotesque and irreligious! Algernon, I forbid you to be baptized. I will not hear of such excesses. Lord Bracknell would be highly displeased if he learned that that was the way in which you wasted your time and money.

CANON CHASUBLE: [*spiritually disappointed but practically relieved*] Am I to understand then that there are to be no christenings at all this afternoon?

JACK: I don't think that, as things are now, it would be of much practical value to either of us, Dr. Chasuble.

CANON CHASUBLE: [*with restrained disapproval*] I am grieved to hear such sentiments from you, Mr. Worthing. They savor of the heretical views of the Anabaptists,[6] views that I have completely refuted in four of my unpublished sermons. However, as your present mood seems to be one peculiarly secular, I will return to the church at once. Indeed, I have just been informed by the pewopener that for the last hour and a half Miss Prism has been waiting for me in the vestry.

LADY BRACKNELL: (*starting*) Miss Prism! Did I hear you mention a Miss Prism?

CANON CHASUBLE: Yes, Lady Bracknell. I am on my way to join her.

---

[6] A Christian sect which rejected infant baptism. Its adherents were therefore often rebaptized at a mature age.

LADY BRACKNELL: Pray allow me to detain you for a moment. This matter may prove to be one of vital importance to Lord Bracknell and myself. Is this Miss Prism a female of repellent aspect, remotely connected with education?

CANON CHASUBLE: (*somewhat indignantly*) She is the most cultivated of ladies, and the very picture of respectability.

LADY BRACKNELL: It is obviously the same person. May I ask what position she holds in your household?

CANON CHASUBLE: (*severely*) I am a celibate, madam.

JACK: (*interposing*) Miss Prism, Lady Bracknell, has been for the last three years Miss Cardew's esteemed governess and valued companion.

LADY BRACKNELL: In spite of what I hear of her, I must see her at once. Let her be sent for.

CANON CHASUBLE: (*looking off*) She approaches; she is nigh.

Miss Prism enters hurriedly.

MISS PRISM: [*reproachfully*] I was told you expected me in the vestry, dear Canon. I have been waiting for you there for an hour and three-quarters. (*catches sight of Lady Bracknell, who has fixed her with a stony glare. Miss Prism grows pale and quails. She looks anxiously round as if desirous to escape.*)

LADY BRACKNELL: (*in a severe, judicial voice*) Prism! (*Miss Prism bows her head in shame.*) Come here, Prism! (*Miss Prism approaches in a humble manner.*) Prism! Where is that baby? (*General consternation. The Canon starts back in horror. Algernon and Jack pretend to be anxious to shield Cecily and Gwendolen from hearing the details of a terrible public scandal.*) Twenty-eight years ago, Prism, you left Lord Bracknell's house, Number 104 Upper Grosvenor Street, in charge of a perambulator that contained a baby, of the male sex. You never returned. A few weeks later, through the elaborate investigations of the Metropolitan police, the perambulator was discovered at midnight, standing by itself in a remote corner of Bayswater.[7] It contained the manuscript of a three-volume novel of more than usually revolting sentimentality. (*Miss Prism starts in involuntary indignation.*) But the baby was not there! (*Everyone looks at Miss Prism.*) Prism, where is the baby? (*A pause.*)

MISS PRISM: [*shamefacedly*] Lady Bracknell, I admit with shame that I do not know. I only wish I did. The plain facts of the case are these. On the morning of the day you mention, a day that is forever branded on my memory, I prepared as usual to take the baby out in its perambulator. I had also with me a somewhat old but capacious hand-bag in which I had intended to place the manuscript of a work of fiction that I had written during my few unoccupied hours. In a moment of mental abstraction, for which I can never forgive myself, I deposited the manuscript in the bassinet,[8] and placed the baby in the hand-bag.

JACK: (*who has been listening attentively*) But where did you deposit the hand-bag?

MISS PRISM: [*with trembling reticence*] Do not ask me, Mr. Worthing.

JACK: [*with slightly frantic urgency*] Miss Prism, this is a matter of no small importance to me. I insist on knowing where you deposited the hand-bag that contained that infant.

MISS PRISM: [*faintly*] I left it in the cloak-room of one of the larger railway stations in London.

JACK: [*peremptorily*] What railway station?

MISS PRISM: (*quite crushed*) Victoria. The Brighton line. (*She sinks into a chair.*)

JACK: [*his eyes dancing with illumination*] I must retire to my room for a moment. Gwendolen, wait here for me.

GWENDOLEN: [*meltingly*] If you are not too long, I will wait here for you all my life.

Jack goes off [*to the left*] *in great excitement.*

---

[7] An area of London near Kensington Gardens.
[8] A covered perambulator.

CANON CHASUBLE: [*with gentle and dreamy curiosity*] What do you think this means, Lady Bracknell?

LADY BRACKNELL: I dare not even suspect, Dr. Chasuble. I need hardly tell you that in families of high position strange coincidences are not supposed to occur. They are hardly considered the thing. (*Noises heard overhead as if some one was throwing trunks about. Everybody looks up.*)

CECILY: Uncle Jack seems strangely agitated.

CANON CHASUBLE: Your guardian has a very emotional nature.

LADY BRACKNELL: [*instinctively hostile to any form of competition*] This noise is extremely unpleasant. It sounds as if he was having an argument. I dislike arguments of any kind. They are always vulgar, and often convincing.

CANON CHASUBLE: (*looking up*) It has stopped now. (*The noise is redoubled.*)

LADY BRACKNELL: I wish he would arrive at some conclusion.

GWENDOLEN: This suspense is terrible. I hope it will last.

Jack reappears with a hand-bag of black leather in his hand.

JACK: (*rushing over to Miss Prism*) Is this the handbag, Miss Prism? Examine it carefully before you speak. The happiness of more than one life depends on your answer.

MISS PRISM: (*calmly*) It seems to be mine. Yes, here is the injury it received through the upsetting of a Gower Street omnibus in younger and happier days. Here is the stain on the lining caused by the explosion of a temperance beverage, an incident that occurred at Leamington.[9] And here, on the lock, are my initials. I had forgotten that in an extravagant mood I had had them placed there. The bag is undoubtedly mine. [*breaking into an expression of ecstatic beatitude*] I am delighted to have it so

---

[9] A spa town in Warwickshire, near Birmingham.

unexpectedly restored to me. It has been a great inconvenience being without it all these years.

JACK: (*in a pathetic voice*) Miss Prism, more is restored to you than this hand-bag. I was the baby you placed in it.

MISS PRISM: (*amazed*) You?

JACK: (*embracing her*) Yes . . . Mother! [*He fairly blurts out the word.*]

MISS PRISM: (*recoiling in indignant astonishment*) Mr. Worthing! I am unmarried!

JACK: Unmarried! I do not deny that is a serious blow. [*indulgently and with a trace of New Testament benignity*] But after all, who has the right to cast a stone against one who has suffered? Cannot repentance wipe out an act of folly? [*with the sudden shrillness of a crusader for women's rights*] Why should there be one law for men and another for women? Mother, I forgive you. (*He tries to embrace her again.*)

MISS PRISM: (*still more indignant*) Mr. Worthing, there is some error. (*pointing to Lady Bracknell*) There is the lady who can tell you who you really are.

JACK: (*after a pause*) [*and in an abruptly changed tone of quiet, routine curiosity*] Lady Bracknell, I hate to seem inquisitive, but would you kindly inform me who I am?

LADY BRACKNELL: I am afraid that the news I have to give you will not altogether please you. You are the son of my poor sister, Mrs. Moncrieff, and consequently Algernon's elder brother.

JACK: [*in great excitement*] Algy's elder brother! Then I have a brother after all. I knew I had a brother! I always said I had a brother! Cecily—how could you have ever doubted that I had a brother? (*seizes hold of Algernon*) Dr. Chasuble, my unfortunate brother. Miss Prism, my unfortunate brother. Gwendolen, my unfortunate brother. Algy, you young scoundrel, you will have to treat me with more respect in the future. You have never behaved to me like a brother in all your life.

ALGERNON: Well, not till today, old boy, I admit. I did

my best, however, though I was out of practice. (*shakes hands*)

GWENDOLEN: (*to Jack*) My own! But what own are you? What is your Christian name, now that you have become some one else?

JACK: Good heavens! . . . I had quite forgotten that point. Your decision on the subject of my name is irrevocable, I suppose?

GWENDOLEN: I never change, except in my affections.

CECILY: What a noble nature you have, Gwendolen!

JACK: Then the question had better be cleared up at once. Aunt Augusta, a moment. At the time when Miss Prism left me in the hand-bag, had I been christened already?

LADY BRACKNELL: Every luxury that money could buy, including christening, had been lavished on you by your fond and doting parents.

JACK: Then I was christened! That is settled. Now, what name was I given? Let me know the worst.

LADY BRACKNELL: Being the eldest son you were naturally christened after your father.

JACK: (*irritably*) Yes, but what was my father's Christian name?

LADY BRACKNELL: (*meditatively*) I cannot at the present moment recall what the General's Christian name was. But I have no doubt he had one. He was eccentric, I admit. But only in later years. And that was the result of the Indian climate, and marriage, and indigestion, and other things of that kind.

JACK: [*beseechingly*] Algy! Can't you recollect what our father's Christian name was?

ALGERNON: My dear boy, we were never even on speaking terms. He died before I was a year old.

JACK: His name would appear in the Army Lists of the period, I suppose, Aunt Augusta?

LADY BRACKNELL: The General was essentially a man of peace, except in his domestic life. But I have no doubt his name would appear in any military directory.

JACK: The Army Lists of the last forty years are here.

These delightful records should have been my constant study. (*rushes to bookcase and tears the books out*) [*A stage tradition has him mount a stepladder to get the books from a high shelf of the built-in bookcase. He sits on the ladder as he examines the records.*] M. Generals ... Mallam, Maxbohm. Magley, what ghastly names they have—Markby, Migsby, Mobbs, Moncrieff! Lieutenant 1840, Captain, Lieutenant-Colonel, Colonel, General 1869, Christian names, Ernest John. (*puts book very quietly down and speaks quite calmly*) I always told you, Gwendolen, my name was Ernest, didn't I? Well, it is Ernest after all. I mean it naturally is Ernest.

LADY BRACKNELL: [*reminiscently*] Yes, I remember that the General was called Ernest. I knew I had some particular reason for disliking the name.

GWENDOLEN: [*with deep emotion*] Ernest! My own Ernest! I felt from the first that you could have no other name!

JACK: Gwendolen, it is a terrible thing for a man to find out suddenly that all his life he has been speaking nothing but the truth. Can you forgive me?

GWENDOLEN: [*thoughtfully*] I can. For I feel that you are sure to change.

JACK: My own one!

CANON CHASUBLE: (*to Miss Prism*) Laetitia! (*embraces her*)

MISS PRISM: (*enthusiastically*) Frederick! At last!

ALGERNON: Cecily! (*embraces her*) At last!

JACK: Gwendolen! (*embraces her*) At last!

LADY BRACKNELL: [*with clear disapproval*] My nephew, you seem to be displaying signs of triviality.

JACK: (*with clear conviction*) On the contrary, Aunt Augusta, I've now realized for the first time in my life the vital Importance of Being Earnest.

CURTAIN

BIBLIOGRAPHY

THE PLAYWRIGHT

Lewis Broad, *The Friendships and Follies of Oscar Wilde.* London, New York: Hutchinson & Co., 1954.

St. John Ervine, *Oscar Wilde: A Present Time Appraisal.* London: George Allen & Unwin, Ltd., 1951.

Frank Harris, *Oscar Wilde, His Life and Confessions, together with "Memories of Oscar Wilde" by Bernard Shaw.* New York, 1918.

Richard Le Gallienne, *The Romantic '90's.* London: Putnam & Co., 1951.

The Marquess of Queensbury in collaboration with Percy Colson, *Oscar Wilde and the Black Douglas.* London, New York: Hutchinson & Co., 1949.

Kenneth Pearson, *The Life of Oscar Wilde.* London: Methuen & Co., 1946.

E. Roditi, *Oscar Wilde.* Norfolk, Conn.: New Directions Press, 1947.

Oscar Wilde, *De Profundis,* introduction by Vyvyan Holland. London: Methuen & Co., 1949.

Horace Wyndham, *Speranza, A Biography of Lady Wilde.* London, New York: T. V. Boardman & Co., Ltd., 1951.

THE PLAY

The Importance of Being Earnest, with an introduction by John Gielgud. Melbourne, London, Toronto: William Heinemann, Ltd., (Drama Library), October, 1949.

The Importance of Being Earnest, with drawings by Sheila Jackson. London: The Guy Walls Press, 1948.

The Importance of Being Earnest . . . in Four Acts as Originally Written. New York: The New York Public Library, 1956.

The Original Four-Act Version of The Importance of Being Earnest, with an Explanatory Foreword by Vyvyan Holland. London: Methuen & Co., Ltd., 1957.

THE STAGING

Ralph Dutton, *The Victorian Home; Some Aspects of Nineteenth-Century Taste and Manners.* London: B. T. Batsford, 1954.

Ernest Bradlee Watson, *Sheridan to Robertson: A Study of the Nineteenth-Century Stage.* Cambridge: Harvard University Press, 1926.